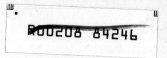

STUDIES IN THE ECONOMIC DEVELOPMENT
OF INDIA

2

CAPITAL FORMATION AND
ECONOMIC DEVELOPMENT

STUDIES IN THE ECONOMIC DEVELOPMENT OF INDIA

CAPITAL FORMATION
AND
ECONOMIC DEVELOPMENT

EDITED BY

P. N. ROSENSTEIN-RODAN

Director of The Indian Project
Center for International Studies
Massachusetts Institute of Technology

THE M.I.T. PRESS
MASSACHUSETTS INSTITUTE OF TECHNOLOGY
CAMBRIDGE   MASSACHUSETTS

PRINTED IN GREAT BRITAIN
in 10 *point Times Roman type*
BY SIMSON SHAND LTD
LONDON, HERTFORD AND HARLOW

CONTENTS

1

THE MATHEMATICAL FRAMEWORK
OF THE
THIRD FIVE YEAR PLAN[1]

S. CHAKRAVARTY

I

The purpose of this paper is threefold:

1. It seeks to formalize the various hypotheses of a systematic nature in models such as have been previously used in Indian development planning. Similar planning models have been used in certain other countries, e.g. the Italian ten-year development plan, and are used at present by Messrs Pant and Little in their respective memoranda concerning the forthcoming Indian Plan. In thus formalizing, it reveals the essential interconnections implicit in the planning calculations, e.g. the way in which the various exogenous and endogenous variables hang together, once certain basic parameter values have been assumed to be known.

2. Having drawn up the formal scheme or the 'model', if we prefer to use this expression, several numerical illustrations are presented in the following order:

    (i) The Pant-Little case using their model structure and parameter values;

    (ii) The modified Pant-Little case with a capital coefficient equal to 3;

    (iii) The same case with an increased amount of foreign aid, all the assumed parameter values being the same as in (ii).

These comparisons will serve the important purpose of highlighting the degree of economic realism implicit in these numerical exercises.

[1] Numerical models as well as the question of 'resource gap' relating to the Third Five Year Plan are discussed in *Alternative Numerical Models of the Third Five Year Plan of India* by Professor P. N. Rosenstein-Rodan. I am indebted to Professors P. N. Rosenstein-Rodan and R. S. Eckaus for valuable suggestions.

3. Once the implications of the model as it stands have been sufficiently worked out, the natural thing to do would be to suggest some simple extensions, particularly when the original version is an overly simple one. We try to indicate a few of the extensions that would make the model a more realistic one from the point of view of decision-making in the present Indian context.

II

Before taking up the various structural equations constituting the type of model generally involved in such plans, it may be useful to add some methodological observations concerning its general nature.

To start with, it should be borne in mind that the model we are after is a type of decision model. This implies that it must necessarily have more unknowns than equations. In other words, the system must possess certain 'degrees of freedom'. The reason for this is that a model which is completely 'locked' (e.g. one for which the number of equations is the same as that of unknowns) cannot serve as a decision model since it cannot discriminate between the results of alternative policy constellations.[1,2] The models implicit in the previous Indian plans as well as the Pant-Little papers satisfy this criterion of having some open ends and hence must be regarded as decision models.

In the usual literature on 'decision models', a distinction is normally drawn between models having fixed targets and those having flexible targets. In the fixed targets case, certain values are ascribed by the planners to the target variables they have in mind. The optimization procedure is generally hidden behind these specified target values. In the flexible targets case, however, the optimization procedure is an integral part of the planning problem. The problem is determinate only after the optimization procedure has been worked out. In general, the flexible targets problem is more difficult to work out than the fixed targets problem and thus, in many planning situations,

---

[1] Each policy constellation is defined by the way the degrees of freedom are filled up.

[2] Any 'locked' model may be easily 'unlocked' by just dropping one equation. Whether it is meaningful to do so depends on the economic nature of the model.

fixed targets are chosen as best indicative of the planners' preferences. The type of model we shall be discussing here is one having fixed targets.

Further, such models are normally linear. This implies that the relationships indicate the constancy of marginal quantities like marginal savings rate, etc. while they may or may not imply constancy of the average quantities. This is not a very restrictive assumption if one confines oneself to a limited period of time, as is usually done in many of these plans.

Finally, although the model is concerned with a period of five years, the present orientation is towards results achieved over the whole period, rather than any year-to-year variation. Thus, even if it is possible in principle to cast the model in terms of difference equations, it is more useful to present it in the form of a set of algebraic equations in which only the initial and final values are related. No essential feature of the model would be lost in this form of presentation.

We have the following variables:

(1) I : total investment
(2) S_t : savings in period 't'
(3) F : the amount of 'net' foreign aid
(4) ΔY : the increase of income over the five-year period
(5) D_A : demand for agricultural output
(6) ΔY_A : increase in agricultural production
(7) T_t : total amount of tax revenue in year 't'
(8) T_t' : part of tax revenue dependent on income or some component of income
(9) ΔY_{NA} : non-agricultural production
(10) C_t : consumption in period 't'
(11) E_t : total Government expenditure over the period
(12) D : increase in Government debt, tax rates remaining unchanged
(13) I_A : investment in agriculture
(14) I_{NA} : investment in non-agriculture
(15) a : the annual increment in savings

The following are the data of the system:

(a) P_t : population in year 't'
(b) $E_{c,t}$: Government current expenditure in period 't'

13

(c) R_t : operating surplus from public enterprises in period 't'

(d) T''_t : the part of tax revenue which is roughly autonomous with respect to income

The data of the system are those variables which are always determined from outside the model.

We have the following set of parameters:

(a) β : the global output-capital ratio

(b) β_a : the output-capital ratio in agriculture

(c) ρ_1 : the proportion of investment expenditure undertaken by the Government

(d) $\gamma_1, \gamma_2, \gamma_3$: the proportions in which existing tax revenue is earned from current consumption, current agricultural income and non-agricultural incomes

(e) η : the income elasticity of demand for agricultural production

We have the following set of equations:

(1) $I = \Sigma I_t = \Sigma S_t + F$

(2) $\Delta Y = \beta I$

(3) $S_t = S_o + t \, a$

(4) $D_A(t) = P_t \left(\dfrac{Y}{P}\right)^\eta_t$

(5) $\Delta Y_A = \beta_a I_A$

(6) $T_t = T'_t + T''_t$

(7) $T_t{}^d = C_t^{\gamma_1} Y_{NA}^{(t)\,\gamma_2} Y_A^{(t)\gamma_3}$

(8) $\Sigma E_t = \Sigma E_c, t + \rho_1 I$

(9) $\Delta D = \Sigma E_t - (\Sigma T_t + \Sigma R_t)$

(10) $\Delta Y_A + \Delta Y_{NA} = \Delta Y$

(11) $I = I_A + I_{NA}$

(12) $\Delta C_t + \Delta S_t = \Delta Y_t$

(13) $\Delta D_A = \Delta Y_a$

Thus we have 15 unknowns and 13 equations. Of these 13 equations (1), (6), (9), (10), (11) are either definitional equations or balance equations, while the remaining are composed of behaviour equations, technological equations, or institutional equations (e.g. tax equations). The above counting shows that the system has two degrees of freedom. The values of any two variables may, therefore, be set arbitrarily from outside, and the remaining variables will be determined from within the system. This gives us a number of alternative policy constellations from which a choice may be made. In the Pant-Little case, these two open ends were filled up by assuming I and F to be given from outside. Certain other possibilities of filling up the open ends are discussed later towards the end of this section.

The following explanations may be offered regarding the structural equations, although a large number of them are self-explanatory. Equation (1) states that total investment over the whole period is equal to total domestic savings plus net foreign aid. Equation (2) indicates the increase in national income over the whole five-year period as obtained from investment over the period multiplied by the incremental output-capital ratio. Equation (3) is a more interesting one. It gives savings at time 't' as a linearly increasing function of time 't', starting from a certain base period. This is just the mathematical equivalent of the numerical projection made in the Pant paper. Although it looks quite arbitrary in itself, taken together with other equations, it defines, although implicitly, how savings change with respect to change in income. Thus the marginal savings propensity is a derived figure. Equation (4) indicates that demand for agricultural production is a function of the level of population as well as the per capita income. Thus, on the logarithmic axis, this will read as follows:

$$\frac{\Delta D_a}{D_a} = \frac{\Delta P}{P} + \eta \frac{\Delta(\frac{Y}{P})}{Y/P}$$

In other words, relative increase in demand for agriculture is the sum of the relative rate of increase in population plus the relative rate of increase in per capita income multiplied by the income-elasticity of demand.

Interpretation of equation (5) is similar to that of equation (2). It may be regarded as a supply equation for agriculture. Equation (6) states that total tax revenue is composed of those taxes which show the same rate of increase as income or some components of income and those which remain roughly invariant with respect to income. Note, however, that this

15

equation presupposes the existing taxes as well as the tax rates to remain unchanged. Equation (7) may be more meaningfully stated in incremental form:

$$\frac{\Delta T'}{T'} = \gamma_1 \frac{\Delta C}{C} + \gamma_2 \frac{\Delta Y_{NA}}{Y_{NA}} + \gamma_3 \frac{\Delta Y_A}{Y_A}$$

In other words, the relative rate of increase in derived tax revenue is equal to the weighted average of the rates at which consumption, agricultural income, and non-agricultural income are increasing, the weights being the proportions in which the existing derived tax revenue is earned from current consumption, current agricultural income, and current non-agricultural income. This approximates very closely the arithmetical procedure used by Little in computing the amount of derived tax revenue, although there is a slight discrepancy in as much as a few items of excise revenue are projected on a somewhat different assumption. Equation (8) describes total Government expenditure over the period as equal to the sum of current expenditure plus the proportion of total investment expenditure that is to be undertaken by the Government. ρ_1 is naturally a policy parameter. The total increase in Government debt is by definition equal to the total expenditure minus total tax revenue and total amount of operating surpluses of public enterprise. This expression has to be modified if we assume that part of the deficits will be covered by introducing new taxes and/or increasing the rate of existing taxes. This implies adding a separate equation to indicate the tax revenues from new sources.

The next three equations are clearly definitional equations in incremental form. The final equation is an equilibrium relation that enables one to decide how total investment will have to be distributed between agriculture and non-agriculture, by equating incremental demand to incremental supply. Since no systematic hypothesis is made concerning the distribution of non-agricultural investment within the different sub-sectors constituting the non-agricultural sector, no additional equations are given.

We shall take up the investment alleviation problem once again when discussing the possibilities of extending the above decision model.

16

It has been remarked previously that we can arbitrarily choose any two of the variables as exogenous and accordingly work out the values of the remaining variables. We may choose among the following possibilities; these are naturally a sample of all the possibilities that exist:

(a) ΔY given and R prescribed from outside. In this case I will be determined as a consequence and so also will be the marginal savings rate.

(b) ΔY given, and the savings programme is prescribed, namely, α, the required amount of foreign aid and the total amount of investment appears as derived magnitudes.

(c) I and F are 'given' from outside. In this case the rate of growth of income, etc. and the marginal savings ratio will be determined in consequence. A few other examples could be given, but the above is sufficiently indicative of what we may do by varying the model. In addition, parameter values may also be assumed to be different from case to case.

III

Let us take up the numerical illustrations of the above algebraic setup.

The following situations will be considered:

(a) the Pant-Little case
- (i) Exogenous variables   I = 10,000 crores
                           F =   1,000 crores
- (ii) Initial values Y_0 = 12,500 crores
                           S_0 =   1,050 crores
- (iii) Parameters

$$\eta = \cdot 75$$
$$\beta = \cdot 45$$
$$\rho_1 = \cdot 67$$
$$\gamma_1 = \cdot 567$$
$$\gamma_2 = \cdot 323$$
$$\gamma_3 = \cdot 007$$

Derivation:
$$I = \Sigma S_t + F$$
$$\therefore \Sigma S_t = 9,000$$
$$\therefore \quad = 5 S_0 + 15 X = 9,000$$
$$\therefore \quad \alpha = 250$$

$\therefore \Delta S = 1,250$

$\Delta Y = \cdot45 \times 10,000$

$= 4,500$. This implies that the relative rate of growth of income per annum is 6 per cent and

$$\frac{\Delta S}{\Delta Y} = \frac{1,250}{4,500} = 28 \text{ per cent}$$

It should be obvious from the calculations that $\dfrac{\Delta S}{\Delta Y} = \dfrac{5\alpha}{\beta I}$

Thus it is determined once α, β, and I are determined. From the above it follows that

$$\frac{\Delta C}{C} = \frac{Y - S}{Y_o - S_o} = \frac{3,250}{11,500} = 28 \text{ per cent.}$$

This implies that the relative rate of growth of consumption per annum is 5 per cent.

Since population is assumed to increase at a rate of 2 per cent per annum, per capita national income increases at 4 per cent per annum. Increase in the demand for agricultural production per annum is equal to $\cdot75 \times \cdot04 + \cdot02 = \cdot05$ or 5 per cent per annum. Agricultural production thus must increase by 5 per cent. This means an increase of non-agricultural production by roughly 7 per cent. Relative increase in derived tax revenue is a weighted average of the rates of growth of consumption, agricultural output and non-agricultural output. With the above values of the rates of growth and the given values of γ_1, γ_2, γ_3, it works out at roughly 6 per cent per annum.

This together with the estimates of autonomous tax revenue gives nearly the total of 6,568 crores over the five-year period. There is, however, a slight discrepancy in as much as Little projects a few of the indirect taxes on bases somewhat different from the above. The difference, however, is negligible in relation to the totals involved.

Putting $\Sigma E_t = 15,700$ crores and $\Sigma T_t + \Sigma R_t$ equal to nearly 9,000 crores, it follows that the balance of Rs. 6,700 crores has to come from borrowing if no new taxes are introduced or the existing tax rates are not increased. Assuming further that external borrowing amounts to 1,000 crores, we are left with the remainder of Rs. 5,700 crores. This total will presumably be distributed into three parts: additional taxes, borrowing, and the 'deficit financing' so called. Interesting questions arise in this connection as how best to fill this gap in the required amount of resources.

Since this problem is already considered in the paper on 'Alternative Models of the Third Five Year Plan of India', we shall not discuss it here.

(b) For the second case, exogenous variables: the same as before

initial values: the same

parameter values: $\beta = \cdot 33$

all other parameters remain unchanged.

ΔY in this case is equal to Rs. 3,300 crores. This implies that national income grows at the rate of 4·8 per cent per annum. Per capita national income goes up at the rate of 2·8 per cent per annum.

$$\frac{\Delta S}{\Delta Y} \frac{5\alpha}{\beta I}$$ since $\Sigma S_t = 9,000$ crores as before, it follows that α is

equal to Rs. 250 crores. Thus,

$$\frac{\Delta S}{\Delta Y} = \frac{1,250}{3,300} = \cdot 38 \text{ or } 38 \text{ per cent annum.}$$

Hence, $$\frac{\Delta C}{C} = \frac{\Delta Y - \Delta S}{C} = \frac{3,300 - 1,250}{11,450} = \frac{2,050}{11,450} = 18 \text{ per cent.}$$

This implies that consumption increases roughly at the rate of 3·5 per cent per annum. Consumption per capita increases at the rate of 1·5 per cent per annum.

Relative increase in agricultural demand $= \cdot 028 \times \cdot 75 + \cdot 02 = \cdot 041$ or 4·1 per cent per annum. Non-agricultural output increases roughly at 5·5 per cent per annum. Relative increase in tax revenue in this case is equal to nearly 4·1 per cent per annum. Total revenue over the whole period in this case amounts to roughly 6,270 crores.

Thus, there is a decline in tax revenue by 300 crores. This is a small amount compared with the total but is significant as a proportion of the incremental tax revenue, which is only 700 crores on the present assumption as against the Pant-Little assumption of 1,000 crores.

The marginal savings ratio implied in this programme is very high indeed and raises questions of feasibility in view of the existing sectoral propensities and the marginal income shares of the different sectors in the proposed investment allocation. This point as well as the related question of 'resources gap' is further elaborated in the paper by P. N. Rosenstein-Rodan.

(c) Exogenous variables: $\quad$ I$=$10,000
$$F= 2,500$$
Initial values: unchanged
Parameter values: $\beta=\cdot33$. The rest as in (a)
Derivations:
$$\Sigma S_t=7,500$$

Hence $\alpha= 150$. Hence $\dfrac{\Delta S}{\Delta Y} =\dfrac{5\alpha}{\beta I}=\dfrac{750}{3,300}=23$ per cent.

National income in this case increases at the rate of 4·8 per cent per annum as in case (b). Per capita income accordingly increases at the rate of 2·8 per cent.

Relative rate of growth of consumption in this case is, however, higher than in case (b) because $\dfrac{\Delta C}{C}=\dfrac{3,300-750}{11,450}$

is roughly 22 per cent. This means that consumption will increase at the rate of 4·1 per cent per annum.

Relative increase in demand for agricultural products is the same as in the case (b), e.g. 4·1 per cent. Tax revenue now increases at a relatively higher rate in as much as the rate of growth of consumption is now higher. Tax revenue increases at the rate of 4·5 per cent per annum. This compares with the 4·1 per cent in the previous case.

Total tax revenue now aggregates, over the whole period, to roughly 6,350 crores. This means a slight improvement over the preceding situation. This present calculation necessarily implies that no new taxes are introduced or tax rates remain unchanged.

Case (c) appears to be somewhat more realistic in as much as the marginal savings ratio is considerably lower and the burden of new taxes needed to balance the Government budget lower.

20

IV

It appears that in the interest of more satisfactory decision-making the model as discussed above should be in a somewhat more disaggregated form. Disaggregation should proceed further both on the horizontal as well as the vertical levels. The horizontal level here refers to the distribution of expenditure between final consumer goods while the vertical relations are those involving input-output considerations.

It may be said that the model so far described deals entirely with relationships on the horizontal level. But even there it is very far from being complete. While the model indicates how an increment of per capita national income will be distributed between food and non-food items, it does not say anything about the distribution of the different items belonging to the food category or of those falling within the non-food category. Demand for consumer goods, particularly textiles and housing services in the urban area, are likely to be the two most important categories on the level of final consumer demand. Insertion of corresponding equations would thus enable us to determine the ratios in which investment should be allocated to these sectors.

Allocating investment resources to sectors whose products are mostly used for interindustrial purposes, namely, those sectors where circularity is apt to be very important, requires information concerning the input-output relations. Even for an underdeveloped country like India a partial input-output analysis may be extremely important when investment is being channelled into the steel-fuel-metal complex. Having estimated the sum total of incremental demand for each of these sectors, the total being composed both of direct and derived demands, we may be in a position to suggest how much should be allocated to these sectors. This is all the more possible because the knowledge of capital-output ratios obtained from the data regarding more advanced countries may be applicable here since the technological process would roughly be the same.

It may, however, be true that in the detailed preparation of the programmes for industrial development these cross-effects have been taken into account in which input-output considerations are implicitly considered. In the present model this will

21

be reflected in the value of the global capital-coefficient. Even so, it may be better to put them more explicitly so as to make for more consistent allocation of investment among the various industrial sectors.

No reference has been made in the above to the employment aspects of the problem. Pant gives an estimate of the incremental employment effects of the investment allocation scheme he suggests. These are essentially derived magnitudes. What is important is that a few of the allocation ratios may be so chosen as to attain certain desired increases in employment. This is possible because, first, the sectors differ with regard to their labour intensity, and, secondly, within some sectors labour intensities of different processes may be different. The employment aspect of the question was one of the main issues of the second plan. It is still important and should not be treated only as a derived phenomenon.

It should also be apparent from the model that the foreign trade aspects of the problem are nowhere explicitly integrated with the other aspects of the economy. As a matter of fact, the model so formulated shows clearly only the inflow of capital that is needed in order to finance the import surplus that is expected to arise over the plan. But how the import surplus is expected to arise is mentioned only very briefly by the plan, and this will undoubtedly be the subject of an additional study. Especially here the choice of investment ratios is of importance in as much as the export-expanding or import-saving industries appear to be particularly important in the present Indian context.

To sum up, if there are 'n' sectors, then there are (n-1) allocation ratios of investment which may be used as (n-1) instruments. It follows from an elementary principle of economic policy that we can attain (n-1) targets with the help of (n-1) instruments. The suggestions above are mainly intended to show how these (n-1) targets may be chosen by means of extending the scope of the present model through incorporating a few new relationships.

2

ALTERNATIVE NUMERICAL MODELS OF THE THIRD FIVE YEAR PLAN OF INDIA[1]

P. N. ROSENSTEIN-RODAN

The purpose of this brief note is to examine the extent to which the various economic magnitudes considered in the Indian Development Programme have to be changed if the capital-output ratio were 3:1 instead of 2·2:1, assumed in both Messrs Pant and I. M. D. Little's memoranda.[2] We shall also consider the ways of financing Indian development if the marginal rate of savings in India were not 27 per cent (and 38 per cent if the capital-output ratio were to be 3:1) as implicitly assumed in the Pant and Little memoranda, but considerably lower, within the range of 20 to 25 per cent (say 23 per cent).

I

Basic Data

National Income	1960-61	Crores	12,500
Total Investment	5 year period	„	10,000
Total Government Expenditure		„	15,700
Public Investment		„	6,700
Current Expenditure		„	9,000

These magnitudes provide the base for three alternative models of development, which are described in the table on the following page.

---

[1] Generalized models are considered in *The Mathematical Framework of the Third Five Year Plan* by S. Chakravarty, who also gave ample assistance in the preparation of the present paper.

[2] See P. Pant, *Dimensional Hypotheses Concerning the Third Five Year Plan* (unpublished), New Delhi, February 1959; I. M. D. Little, *Public Finance and the Third Plan*, M.I.T., New Delhi, May 1959.

23

THREE NUMERICAL MODELS OF INDIAN DEVELOPMENT, 1960–1966

	(a) (Pant-Little) Capital-Output Ratio 2.2:1 Marginal Rate of Savings 28%	*(b)* Capital-Output Ratio 3:1 Marginal Rate of Savings 38%	*(c)* Capital-Output Ratio 3:1 Marginal Rate of Savings 23%
A. 1. National Income 1st year	12,500	12,500	12,500
2. National Income 5th year	17,000	15,800	15,800
3. Increase in National Income 5 years	4,500	3,300	3,300
4. Rate of Growth	6%	4·8%	4·8%
B. 1. Domestic Savings 1st year (% of National Income)	1,050 (8·4%)	1,050	1,050
2. Domestic Savings 5th year (% of National Income)	2,300 (13·4%)	2,300 (15%)	1,800 (11·4%)
3. Domestic Savings over 5 years	9,000	9,000	7,500
C. 1. Increase in Consumption over 5 years	27%	18%	22%
2. Rate of Increase	5%	3·5%	4·1%
3. Rate of Increase per capita	3%	1·5%	2·1%

	(Pant-Little) Capital-Output Ratio 2·2:1 Marginal Rate of Savings 28%	Capital-Output Ratio 3:1 Marginal Rate of Savings 38%	Capital-Output Ratio 3:1 Marginal Rate of Savings 23%
D. 1. Increase in Agricultural Production (assumption of income elasticity of demand [*not* consumers' expenditure elasticity] equal to 0·75)	5%	4·1%	4·1%
E. 1. Taxation Yields	9,600 (9568)	9,600 (9581)	8,500
2. Existing Taxes	6,600 (6568)	6,300 (6270)	6,350[2]
3. New Taxes	3,000	3,300[3] (3311)	2,150[4]
4. Share of Taxes in National Income 1st year	9·8%	9·8%	9·8%
5th year	14·4%	16%	12·5%
5. Government Enterprise Surplus	2,400 (2419)	2,400[1,3] (2419)	2,300[4]
6. Government Borrowing	2,600	2,600[1,3]	2,400[4]
7. Foreign Aid	1,100	1,100	2,500[5]
8. Total Government Expenditure	15,700	15,700	15,700

[1] More difficult to achieve if income increase is smaller (4·8% instead of 6% p.a.).

[2] Existing taxes yield 50 crores more than under (*b*) because consumption increases at the rate of 4% p.a. instead of 3·5%.

[3] The sum total of E 3+5+6 must amount to 8,300 crores. How it is to be distributed among the three items is a matter of policy decision.

[4] The sum total of E 3+5+6 must amount to 6,850 crores. How it is to be distributed among the three items is a matter of policy decision.

[5] We assume foreign aid of 3,000 crores out of which 2,500 available for investment and 1,500 used for converting short- and medium-term credits to a long-run basis.

	1960-61	1961-2	1962-3	1963-4	1964-5	1965-6
F. 1. Government Current Expenditure	1,143	1,211	1,285	1,368	1,463	1,566
2. National Income (*a*) (increase at 6% p.a.)	12,500	13,220	14,030	14,930	15,930	17,000
3. Government Current Expenditure as % of National Income (*a*)	9·1	9·2	9·2	9·2	9·2	9·2
4. National Income (*b* and *c*) (increasing at 4·8%)	12,500	13,030	13,630	14,290	15,020	15,800
5. Government Current Expenditure as % of National Income (*b* and *c*)	9·1	9·3	9·4	9·6	9·7	10
6. Total Government Expenditure (current and investment)	2,043	2,261	2,485	2,708	2,963	3,116
7. National Income (*a*)	12,500	13,220	14,030	14,930	15,930	17,000
8. National Income (*b* and *c*)	12,500	13,030	13,630	14,290	15,020	15,800
9. Total Government Expenditure (National Income *a*)	16%	10·4%	17·7%	18%	18·6%	18·4%
10. Total Government Expenditure (National Income *b* and *c*)	16%	17·4%	18·2%	19%	19·6%	20%

II. MODEL a (CAPITAL-OUTPUT RATIO 2·2:1)

The extent of the changes between models *a* and *b* (and *c*) show how crucial the capital-output ratio is, i.e. how highly other variables depend on its assumed value. If it were 2·2:1, National Income would increase at 6 per cent per annum; the presently existing taxes would yield additional 1,000 crores; additional new taxes might be more easily raised, perhaps even up to the high Pant-Little level of 14·4 per cent of National Income per annum at the end of the five year period, which implies a marginal propensity to tax of 27 per cent. Government borrowing (E 6) of 2,600 crores might also be possible without undue inflationary effect; at any rate it would be less difficult than under assumption *b* when National Income increases at the lower rate of 4·8 per cent per annum. The same applies to the Surplus of Government Enterprises (E 5): it might be achieved with less difficulty when income increases at 6 per cent per annum instead of 4·8 per cent per annum. Even under this optimistic (model *a*) assumption, however, the combined burden of additional taxes, Government Enterprise Surplus, and Government Borrowing (E 3+5+6)—while at the same time savings have to be high and rising from 8·4 per cent per annum up to 13·4 per cent per annum (marginal rate of savings =27 per cent)—may well prove to be excessive. Foreign Aid might have to be increased even under the most optimistic assumption of the low capital-output ratio to fill in not only the 'foreign exchange gap' but also to a marginal extent the 'resources gap'.

The assumption of a capital-output ratio 2·2:1 seems, however, to be dangerously optimistic. The same ratio was wrongly assumed for the Second Five Year Plan. It is admittedly difficult to have for it a reliable estimate and projection. Agriculture provides 50 per cent of G.N.P. in India, and, apart from additional investment and good monsoons on the one hand, and a vigorous organization and drive in agriculture on the other, it may 'make all the difference' whether the increase in agricultural production is to be 5 per cent or half of it. At the same investment level the amount of increase in agricultural production may largely influence whether income will increase at 6, 5, or 4 per cent per annum. But while such 'non-invest-

27

ment' factors may largely influence the capital-output ratio, they do not determine it entirely. The capital-output ratio also depends on the composition of investment, and no special justification for a low capital-output ratio for the Third Five Year Plan in India is discernible. The lags between input and output (gestation periods) in various sectors have to be taken into account. It might be unrealistic, moreover, to count throughout and everywhere on a 'record' performance: gestation periods might in part be somewhat longer in India than in the United States or western Europe. While only a more detailed analysis of possible alternative compositions of investment and of the lags inherent in them could give a more reliable estimate, it seems far more realistic to assume a high capital-output ratio of 3:1.

III. MODEL b

If the capital-output ratio is 3:1, investment of 10,000 crores yields a smaller increase in National Income of 4·8 per cent per annum. In order to mobilize 10,000 crores for investment with only 1,100 crores of Foreign Aid, Taxation, Surplus of Government Enterprises, and Government Borrowing (E 2+3 +5+6) as well as Savings have to be stepped up. Existing taxes (E 2) at the lower increase in income yield 300 crores less than in model a, in which income increased at 6 per cent per annum.[1] Since new taxes of 3,000 crores would have to be raised, taxes would have to rise from 9.8 per cent of National Income, at the beginning of the plan, to 16 per cent at its end, i.e. a marginal propensity to tax of 39 per cent! While this is not easy, it is equally more difficult to realize a Surplus of Government Enterprises of 2,600 crores when National Income rises at the low rate of 4·8 per cent and it is also more difficult to fulfil the target of Government Borrowing of 2,600 crores without undue inflationary effects. All these measures of mobilizing resources for the Government (E 3+5+6) have to be realized while Private Savings are supposed to rise. Additional

---

[1] If income were constant, existing taxes would yield over the Five Year Period 4,170 crores. If income increased at 6 per cent per annum, the yield of existing taxes would increase by 1,000 crores. If income increased at 4·8 per cent per annum, the increase is about 700 crores, i.e. a fall of nearly 30 per cent in additional tax revenue.

Government revenue (E 2+3+5) will originate from increase in output, from consumption, and to some extent—which should be kept to a minimum but which cannot be quite eliminated—from private savings. Total Savings in model *b* are assumed to rise from 8·4 per cent of National Income in the first year to 15 per cent in the fifth—implying a marginal rate of savings of 38 per cent—which seems indeed to be far too heroic a target.

A Discussion of Savings Potentials

The marginal rate of savings is assumed to be constant throughout the five-year period while the average rate of savings will, of course, be rising. While reliable statistical evidence on the formation and flow of savings in India is not available, analogies from other countries may point to plausible assumptions. Savings originate in three sectors: (i) Corporate or Business Sector, (ii) Private Savings, and (iii) Government Savings.

(*i*) In the sector of corporate and business savings a very high marginal rate of 30-40 per cent seems to be institutionally characteristic in India as well as in developed countries. This sector represents, however, only around 3 per cent of Indian national income and perhaps 7 to 9 per cent of national savings. It will grow through time and will represent a higher proportion of Indian income and savings, but even in 1966 it will still be below the share this sector represents in, say, Italy, not to mention the United Kingdom or the United States. The marginal rate of savings in this sector can be assumed to remain consistently high (say 35 per cent) but it seems unlikely that it should be rising.

(*ii*) Private savings, which form the bulk of savings in India, might be considered in two sub-groups of directly invested savings in small unincorporated businesses, trade, industry, and agriculture, and the second sub-group of other personal savings. In the first sub-group the marginal rate of savings will be considerably higher (twice as much or more) than the average rate, say 16 to 20 per cent, as compared with about 35 per cent, in the corporate sector; but the difference between marginal and average rate is likely to fall as the average rate of savings rises. In the second sub-group of personal savings the marginal rate will also be higher than

29

the average rate, say 12 to 15 per cent (compared with 7 to 8 per cent average rate), but the difference between the marginal and average rates may be assumed to be smaller than in the first sub-group, and it is likely to fall as income per head of the average rate of savings rises. When the average rate of personal savings reaches 10 to 12 per cent, the marginal rate may be equal to the average or be only infinitesimally higher. For the sector of private savings as a whole, the marginal rate during the five year period is likely to be much higher than the average rate, but there is no special reason to assume that the marginal rate itself will be rising.

(*iii*) *Government Savings.* A special effort and drive should raise Government savings during the Third Five Year Plan as compared with the Second Five Year Plan. This increase is, however, in the nature of a once and for all movement raising the Government savings from the previous to a higher level; there is no reason to assume a cumulative process whereby the marginal rate of Government savings should be rising from year to year. During the Third Five Year period as compared with the Second Five Year period, the marginal rate will therefore be uniformly higher than the average rate. For total savings the most plausible[1] assumption seems, therefore, to be that the marginal rate will be higher than the average but that this marginal rate itself will be roughly constant through 1961 to 1966. This implies, of course, that the average rate will be rising. Taking the three groups of savings into account, a combined marginal rate may at best be estimated at somewhere between 20 and 25 per cent—say 23 per cent, as considered in model *c*—but it is not very probable that it should reach 27 per cent, not to mention the very high rate of 38 per cent in a nontotalitarian economy without too drastic austerity measures.

How Realistic is Model b?

In fact, model *b* is based on quite unrealistic assumptions. It mainly serves the purpose of a *reductio ad absurdum*: if the capital-output ratio is 3:1—a realistic and plausible assumption —and if foreign aid were to be a mere 1,100 crores, then the

---

[1] While the business sector's small share in income will rise, the share of income of other sectors will not change materially.

investment target of 10,000 crores, which would yield an increase in income of 4·8 per cent per annum, is not likely to be achieved. The strain of mobilizing sufficient Government revenue and sufficient national savings would be excessive. A higher amount of foreign aid seems to be the only way out.

IV. MODEL C

Accordingly, a much higher amount of foreign aid, which alone can secure success in achieving a rate of growth of 4·8 per cent per annum, is assumed here. The estimated required amount is 3,000 crores, out of which 2,500 crores would be available for net investment while 500 crores would be used for converting medium and short-term external debt payments which fall due during this period to a long-term basis. Of the 3,000 crores of foreign aid, about 2,000 will be provided to fill the so-called 'foreign exchange gap'; 1,500 crores are, presumably, a reasonable estimate of the current foreign exchange gap, while 500 crores are needed for the additional foreign exchange gap due to external short- and medium-term debt repayment during this period. 1,000 crores of foreign aid are needed to fill the resources gap. This will allow a rate of increase of consumption per head of 2·1 per cent, keeping the share of taxes in national income to 12·5 per cent at the end of the year, implying a marginal propensity to tax of 23 per cent; it will make it easier to achieve the surplus in Government enterprises of 2,300 crores and Government borrowing of 2,400 crores. It is obvious that the distribution of aid between additional taxes, surplus of Government enterprise, and Government borrowing (E 3+5+6) is a matter of policy and can vary; but the sum total must amount to 6,850 crores. Government current expenditure as percentage of national income (F 5) will be mildly rising from 9·3 per cent in the first year of the plan to 10 per cent in the last year. The share of total Government expenditure (current and public investment) will rise from 17 per cent in the first year to 20 per cent in the last one. At that level it will still be considerably below the level of 25 to 30 per cent characteristic of developed countries in the Free World. A consideration of the three alternative numerical models of the Third Five Year Plan of India seems to us to suggest the conclusion that the third model c, based on the three assumptions of a capital-output ratio of 3:1, of the marginal rate of savings of 23 per cent, and of an amount of foreign aid of 3,000 crores (out of which 2,500 available for net investment), is more realistic than the others.

3

AN OUTLINE OF A METHOD
FOR PROGRAMME EVALUATION[1]

S. CHAKRAVARTY

I. GENERAL DISCUSSION OF THE METHOD

The purpose of the present paper is to outline a method of programme evaluation. Various recent discussions on the so-called 'investment criteria' have had also the same purpose in view, but they have been essentially single-project oriented, with the implicit assumption that a programme could be regarded as a *linear* sum of various individual projects. Thus an optimal programme is assumed to be determined once the priorities of the individual projects are optimally ascertained, each independently of the rest. This, at its best, however, is an insufficient method which, in the absence of decomposability of the programme, could be seriously misleading except in those cases where projects are few and represent a not too significant addition to the existing capital stock. Even then it is not an equivalent to or a substitute for a programme approach.

The method presented here has the following characteristics:

It deals with a whole constellation of interrelated projects rather than a marginal project. With a marginal project it is admissible to use a partial equilibrium approach, involving the cost-benefit ratio or any such criterion, although it may be social cost and social benefit which are involved rather than private cost and private benefit. But the interesting point to note is that any method to determine 'social' as distinguished from private benefit must transcend the possibilities of partial equilibrium approach, thus rendering the usual discussion an

[1] I am greatly indebted to Professor P. N. Rosenstein-Rodan for the suggestion of the problems and his stimulating comments. I am also very grateful to the participants at the M.I.T. India Seminar, in particular to Professors R. S. Eckaus and R. M. Solow for valuable suggestions. The errors that persist are all mine.

inexact one, or simply replacing one set of unknowns by another. An interrelated group of projects necessarily demands a more general approach which emphasizes intersectoral dependence, etc. In certain cases the use of 'shadow prices' to calculate cost-benefit ratios may obviate the necessity for a full-scale programme approach if the shadow prices can be approximated in relatively simple ways.[1]

Secondly, the method is dynamic, inasmuch as the development of the economy over *several* periods of time is an essential part of it, while most of the programme evaluation techniques yield results for a *single* period of time.

Thirdly, the method uses an explicit characterization of the projects involving the ensemble of technical data, i.e. the gestation lags, the depreciation rates, the intersectoral capital-output ratios, the degrees of intersectoral dependence in current production, etc. This is an extension of the ordinary methods where all the relevant information is generally subsumed under one or two headings, i.e. the capital-income ratio or the capital-labour ratio.

Lastly, the balance of payments problem may be taken account of by introducing a side-condition that the excess of total import requirements over total exports should not surpass a certain preassigned magnitude. If the side-condition is effective, it necessarily implies a non-zero shadow rate of exchange.

While these are the main characteristics of the method, let us state explicitly the possibilities with regard to the choice of the basic criterion. Certain alternatives present themselves:

(*a*) If the savings coefficient is already known, our criterion may be stated as one of maximizing the sum of incomes over the specified time horizon. In this case no separate provision for terminal equipment is needed, because whatever maximizes total income also maximizes total investment since one bears a well-defined relation to the other; the same holds *a fortiori* for total consumption over the whole period.

(*b*) If the savings rate is an unknown of the problem, then the criterion may be stated as maximizing the sum of consumption over the whole period, subject to a provision

[1] See the next chapter, 'The Use of Shadow Prices in Programme Evaluation'.

for terminal equipment. In this case our unknowns are not merely the distribution of total investment but also the over-all rate of investment in the economy in each time period.

The choice of criterion (*a*) has the advantage that the planning problem is then decomposed into two consecutive problems: the determination of the over-all savings rate and the determination of the composition of investment. The choice of the savings rate already reflects the decisions regarding the future. It should be understood that the situation holds even though the savings coefficient is not fixed but varies in a predictable manner over time. If it varies with the level of income, then we have a non-linear system which is still a well-determined one. In what follows we shall assume criterion (*a*) on considerations of simplicity.

The procedure for determining this maximum consists in using an arbitrary parameter that indicates how net total investment is distributed between two sectors, which, for convenience, we call the 'programme sector' and the rest of the economy. This bisector classification is only a simplifying device since, as a matter of fact, the two sectors here represent any two sectors that together make up the whole economy. In a more disaggregated approach it will be necessary to have 'n' sectors where n >2. Although the computational difficulties are increased, the method outlined here is equally applicable to the more general situation. In the two sector case there is only one independent allocation coefficient, 'λ', which indicates how net total investment is to be distributed between two sectors, while in the 'n'-sector case we have (n-1) such as 'λ's'. In the two sector case the single 'λ' is to be so determined as to satisfy our basic criterion, while in the 'n'-sector case the criterion requires the determination of an optimal configuration of (n-1) λ's.

The following algebraic model gives an answer to the above problem of maximization on a first level of approximation. This model will be extended in Section III to take into account the following questions:

1. The direct (nonmarket) technological externalities which make output or increment of output in any particular sector dependent not merely on the capital or increment

35

of capital invested in these respective sectors but also on capital invested in other sectors.

2. The changes in the flow coefficients (a_{1j}), which are the Leontief coefficients for cross-deliveries, normally associated with an expanding size of the industry. The simplest way of introducing this factor is to make the input-output relationship 'linear' rather than 'proportional' as is normally done. Thus, if $X_{1j}=a_{1j}X_j+\overline{K}_{1j}$, where $\overline{K}_{1j}$ is a constant, then $\dfrac{X_{1j}}{X_j}$ rises with increasing X_j if $\overline{K}_{1j}<0$; it falls with increasing X_j if $\overline{K}_{1j}>0$. The latter situation corresponds to the phenomenon of increasing returns. Introducing this two-parameter production function renders the Leontief system nonhomogeneous, but it can still be handled in an easy way. For more complicated situations we may introduce cost functions in each input which are either linear or proportional in facets. If proportionality in facets is assumed as realistic, then there must exist certain nodal points of output at which the coefficients change discontinuously. Thus the variability of coefficients is introduced in a way that does not presuppose abandoning completely the traditional apparatus of input-output analysis.

3. Depreciation rates may also be assumed to be variable over time. Thus we may assume relatively lower rates for the initial years and enlarged ones for later years. Secondly we need not adhere to the method of straight-line depreciation, which in a growing economy understates the amount of net investable resources. Thus the usual Domar type of question may be taken care of by changing the depreciation procedure. The more intractable point regarding depreciation that arises in the context of quality change does not appear here because we normally abstract from technical progress in this context.

36

II. AN ALGEBRAIC MODEL

(1) $I(t) = S(t) - D(t)$ Where $I(t)$ is investment at time 't'

$S(t)$ is gross savings at time 't'

and $D(t)$ is depreciation of capital stock at 't'.

In those cases where there is a planned balance of payments deficit, that fact may also be introduced on the right hand side as an additive factor. For simplicity we ignore it for the time being.

We use the following notation:

$V_k(t)$ = Gross output of kth industry at time 't'.

b_k = Output (gross)—capital ratio of the kth industry (direct capital coefficient).

$K_k(t)$ = Capital stock of the kth industry.

$d_k(t)$ = The rate of depreciation of a unit of capital stock in the kth industry.

$\quad$ s = The savings coefficient for the whole economy. We may, if we so prefer, assume this coefficient to be variable from sector to sector. Further, if we are not interested in explicit solutions, we may assume savings coefficients to be variable. This means that the savings ratio diminishes with increase in income. For purposes of numerical extrapolation, this does not raise any additional difficulties.

Equation (1) may then be written as:

$$I(t) = [sY(t) - \overline{d_1 K_1(t) + d_2 K_2(t)}]$$
$$= [s\Sigma \overline{V(t)} - \Sigma\Sigma V_{kk}'(t) - \overline{d_1 K_1(t) + d_2 K_2(t)}]$$
$$= [s\Sigma \overline{b_1 K_1(t)} - \Sigma\Sigma a_{1j} b_j K_j(t) - \overline{d_1 K_1(t) + d_2 K_2(t)}]$$

Now $\lambda_1 I(t)$ is the fraction of net investment that goes to Sector I while $\lambda_2 I(t)$ is the fraction that goes to Sector II, with the natural restriction that $\lambda_1 + \lambda_2 = 1$.

Thus $\lambda_1 I(t) = \lambda_1 [s\Sigma b_i \overline{K_i(t)} - \overline{\Sigma\Sigma a_{1j} b_j K_j(t)} - \overline{d_1 K_1(t) + d_2 K_2(t)}]$
and $\lambda_2 I(t) = (1 - \lambda_1) [\ldots$ same as above $\ldots]$

In the presence of gestation lags there are several ways of indicating evolution of productive capacity over time. We may take the following two cases:

(a) $K_1(t+l_1)-K_1(t+l_1-1)=\lambda_1 I(t)$

$K_2(t+l_2)-K_2(t+l_2-1)=\lambda_2 I(t)$

when l_1 and l_2 are the lags of the two sectors.

(b) A more explicit approach to the problem may be to consider the following case which distinguishes between investment in execution and investment that is finished (which means the *net* rate of increase in capital stock, i.e. addition to capital stock—attrition of capital).[1]

$$I(t)=\frac{1}{l_1}\int_{t}^{t+l_1} I'_1(t)dt \text{ where } I'_1(t) \text{ is investment that is finished}$$

$$=\frac{1}{l_1}\int^{l_1} \dot{K}_1(t)dt=\frac{1}{l_1}[K_1(t+l_1)-K_1(t)]$$

Now we have the following system of equations:

$$K_1(t_1+l_1)-K_1(t)=l_1\lambda_2[s\{\overline{\Sigma b_1 K_1(t)-\Sigma\Sigma a_{1j}b_j K_j(t)}\}$$

$$-\overline{d_1 K_1(t)+d_2 K_2(t)}]$$

$$K_2(t_2+l_2)-K_2(t)=l_2\lambda_1[s\overline{\Sigma b_1 K_1(t)-\Sigma\Sigma a_{1j}b_j K_j(t)}$$

$$-\overline{d_1 K_1(t)+d_2 K_2(t)}]$$

This is a system of linear difference equations of order '1' where $l=\max(l_1, l_1)$. The number of initial conditions needed to start the system is at most $(2\times l)$.

In certain singular cases the system may be 'collapsed' to yield a single difference equation in aggregate capital stock, the order remaining the same as in the 'noncollapsed' state.

Once the $K_1(t)$'s are known as solutions of the system of difference equations as outlined above, the time path of 'Y' and hence the integral of 'Y' over the planning horizon is known too.

Thus the criterion (a) will them imply 'max y' where $y=\int_{o}^{n}Y(t)dt$.

---

[1] This is not a very satisfactory method of dealing with problems of depreciation in the context of gestation lags. However, for the purpose of the present paper the simplicity of this presentation is an advantage which is well worth retaining.

Thus the decision variables λ's will have to be chosen in such a way as to reach the above maximum.

The criterion (b) will imply: max $C = \int_0^n C(t)dt$ subject to $K_n = \overline{K}$. In this case the decision variables are not merely the λ's but include the savings coefficient as well. This naturally is a more complicated problem. The converse to this problem has been considered by Mr Little, who assumes the following criterion: max K_n subject to assuming $C(t) = \overline{C}(t)$, a prescribed function of time.[1]

Assuming continuous derivatives, etc. the maximum in (a) is attained where:

$$\frac{d\overline{y}}{d\lambda_1} = 0, \frac{d^2\overline{y}_2}{d\lambda_1} < 0.$$

In practice the above formalism has hardly much importance since, firstly, it is quite unlikely that the functions involved will have the necessary continuity properties and, secondly, the explicit solution of the difference equations may be quite a job in itself. Thus the technique of 'numerical extrapolation' will have to be employed to trace the development over time. This technique is further considered in an appendix.

The method of numerical extrapolation has the additional advantage that the coefficients need not be assumed to be constant over time. While it is still possible to handle in a somewhat general way a system of linear difference equations with variable coefficients over time, the practical difficulties may be great and the purist may also insist at the same time on convergence proofs, etc. No such problem arises if we adopt what has been called the technique of 'numerical extrapolation'. Thus the technique suggested above may take into account such delayed effects as are normally associated with investments in social overhead capital, etc.

The demand considerations relating to final consumer goods are not gone into in detail in the model presented above. But

[1] See I. M. D. Little, *Reflections on the Theory and Practice of Planning in India* (Cambridge, Mass., Center for International Studies, M.I.T., 1959), which preceded the paper included in this volume, entitled 'The Real Cost of Labor, and the Choice between Consumption and Investment'.

they may also be introduced as additional constraints in a multisectoral model. In that case the set of decision variables will be 'n-r-1' where 'r' is the number of additional equations introduced to take care of certain requirements on the composition of consumption. Thus, if we assume a situation where minimum amounts of consumption of certain commodities have been specified by the planner, a number of decision variables will have to assume a set of values such that technology would enable these required amounts of consumption output to be produced. This limits the range of variability of the set λ's, but there would be a certain amount of freedom so long as the number of restrictions 'r' is less than (n-1). Instead of using the elimination procedure, we may use a more symmetric procedure such as the technique of Lagrange multipliers which maximizes a target function involving λ's subject to the various *a priori* restrictions.[1]

III. SECOND APPROXIMATION OF THE MODEL

We now introduce the changes in our model announced towards the end of Section I.

It should be noted that the introduction of technological interactions requires the use of a new matrix of coefficients which is different from the Leontief matrices so far used. The two Leontief matrices are the matrix of flow coefficients (a_{ij}) and the matrix of investment coefficients (b_{ij}). The Leontief matrix (a_{ij}) is quite explicit in our system of calculations, but the second Leontief matrix is hidden behind the 'b_k's'. Of course $1/b_k$'s are nothing but the column sums of Leontief's second matrix. Thus:

$$\frac{1}{b_k} = \sum_{i=1}^{n} C_{1k}$$

where C_{1k}'s are the intersectoral capital-output ratios.

Now let us assume that $V_1(t) \neq f(K_1)$, and instead $V_1(t) = f(K_1, K_2, \ldots, K_n)$. For simplicity we have

$$V_1(t) = g_{11}K_1 + g_{21}K_2 + \ldots + g_{n1}K_n$$

[1] The discussion in this paper is exclusively devoted to a closed economy. In an open economy, where target setting involves questions of import substitution, more complicated problems may arise. For this, see the author's *The Logic of Investment Planning* (Amsterdam, North Holland Publishing Company, 1959), Chapters V–VII.

$$\text{where } (g_{ij}) = \begin{bmatrix} g_{11} & \cdots & \cdots & \cdots & g_{1n} \\ g_{21} & \cdots & \cdots & \cdots & g_{2n} \\ g_{n1} & \cdots & \cdots & \cdots & g_{nn} \end{bmatrix}$$

Now only $g_{ii} = \dfrac{1}{b_i}$ while the other coefficients g_{ij}, $i \neq j$ are the non-market influence exercised by the ith industry over j^{th} industry. These influences must necessarily be nonmarket influences. To the extent they are taken care of by the market mechanism through the prices and quantities of investment goods and intermediate goods output, they have no place here. The reason for that is the use of two other matrices, (a) and (b), which relate to observable market transactions. Leontief's use of constant coefficients for these matrices, however, precludes any emergence of pecuniary external economies because relative prices remain constant. Thus Leontief can take account only of quantity effects and not of price effects. Pecuniary external economies are, however, considered in our system because (a) we do not assume the technological coefficients to remain unchanged, since they change in facets, and (b) because we have more than one primary factor. It is easy to see that either of these factors is sufficient to introduce pecuniary external economies into the picture. It should, however, be noted that for the system as a whole it is misleading to call such price induced effects 'external'.[1]

The rows of the 'g' matrix indicate the influence exerted by one sector over all the other sectors, while the columns indicate the influence received by one sector from all the other sectors. In ordinary discussion the matrix 'g' is a diagonal matrix so that all the other elements are necessarily zero. The literature on external economies, however, indicates the importance of

[1] Although the pecuniary external economies are internal to the system as a whole and merely reflect the laws of general interdependence of the economy, since the private investor is not in a position to estimate these changes accurately, the investment equilibrium of the economy is affected. On this point, see T. Scitovsky, 'Two Concepts of External Economies', *The Journal of Political Economy*, Vol. LXII (1954).

41

assuming that some off-diagonal elements are not necessarily zero. This does not mean that we have any fool-proof method of estimating these coefficients. In the first place it is necessary to consider whether these coefficients are 'identifiable' in the sense the term is used in econometric literature. What kind of *a priori* restrictions on the 'structure' of the system are necessary in order to render them identifiable? This is all the more important if we have technical progress, because then the distinction between technological external economies and the over-all effect of technical progress is a somewhat blurred one in practice. But conceptually the literature on economic development has often maintained, and rightly, that certain industries act more frequently as transmitters of growth via the effect that they have on the productivity of labour, thus providing an instance of technological externality. Although labour is not formally in our equation, its influence is taken account of through the shape of the equations or the values of the coefficients. The off-diagonal elements crucial to the present argument are those referring to the 'g' matrix. The presence or absence of off-diagonal elements in the other matrices (*a* and *b*) are indicative of triangularity in the processes of production and capital formation.[1] It is generally held that there are certain sectors of the economy which are important from the point of view of radiating influence on all the other sectors, and they are normally classified as belonging to the 'infrastructure'.

Having discussed the general nature of this new matrix, we now rework our set of difference equations for this modified case. We assume $n=2$ for the sake of exposition. The equations are now as follows:

$$K_1(t+1_1) - K_1(t) = l_1\lambda_1[s\,\{\overline{g_{11}K_1(t) + g_{21}K_2(t) + g_{12}K_1(t)}$$
$$+ \overline{g_{22}K_2(t)}$$
$$- \overline{(a_{12}V_2(t) + a_{21}V_1(t)}\} - \overline{d_1K_1(t) + d_2K_2(t)}]$$
$$= l_1\lambda_1[s\,\{\overline{(g_{11}+g_{12})K_1(t) + (g_{21}+g_{22})K_2(t)}$$
$$- \overline{(a_{12}g_{12}K_1(t) + a_{12}g_{22}K_2(t) + a_{21}g_{11}K_1(t)}$$
$$+ \overline{a_{21}g_{21}K_2(t)}\} - \overline{d_1K_1(t) + d_2K_2(t)}]$$

[1] The triangularity in the (a) matrix is significant also from a computational point of view. This is so because only the matrix $(I-a)$ is needed for inversion.

$$K_1(t+l_1)=\lambda_1 l_1 [s\ \overline{\{(g_{11}+g_{12})}=s\overline{(a_{12}g_{12}+a_{21}g_{11})}-d_1\}\ K_1(t)$$
$$+\{s\overline{(g_{21}+g_{22})}-s\overline{(a_{12}g_{22}+a_{21}g_{21})}-d_2\}\ K_2(t)]+K_1(t)$$
$$K_2(t+l_2)=\lambda_2 l_2\ [\ .\ .\ .\ \text{same as above}\ .\ .\ .\ ]+K_2(t).$$

Thus we have a system of two difference equations, the order being $l=\max(l_1, l_2)$, as in the previous case. Once again, we may try to solve the case explicitly or attempt the method of numerical extrapolation as mentioned earlier.

While the method proposed above formally takes into account the technological externalities so far as the evolution of output and productive capacity are concerned, there are very difficult problems of estimation involved: as remarked previously, the 'g' coefficients are not easily determined.[1]

We now turn to the second of the major extensions. This relates to the way in which the variability in time of the coefficients of the two Leontief matrices may be incorporated in our model. One way of introducing such variability is to assume these coefficients to be autonomous functions of time. In other words, the sole reason why the coefficients change is technical progress. Thus differences between coefficients at two different points of time are indicative of 'structural change' due to innovations, etc. This, however, is a cheap way of generalization unless we can foresee the nature and extent of such technical progress, which is bound to be quite difficult to predict. To the extent technical progress is correctly foreseen, we may incorporate them into our model without difficulty. While technical progress is not easily foreseen, the variability introduced into the picture via the increasing outputs of different industries over time can be more easily projected. These changes reflect the economies of scale which become important when the industry has reached a certain size as well as the Allyn Young type of external economies due to greater size of the market. A cross-section study of the production functions of comparable industries in different countries at

---

[1] In this connection, it is interesting to note that the parametrization device generally connected with the dual of a programming becomes very complicated in the presence of externalities. The problem has been discussed against the background of statistical considerations. Nothing has been done in the literature in this dynamic setting. For a discussion of the static question, see F. M. Bator, 'The Anatomy of Market Failure', *The Quarterly Journal of Economics*, Vol. LXXII (1958).

different stages of growth may indicate how the relevant coefficients change when the size of output increases. A study of this nature has already been undertaken by Chenery.[1] Such a study is quite indispensable from the operational point of view if variability of coefficients is to be introduced into planning questions. At this stage the transition in our analysis should be carefully paced. Thus our first extension consists only in introducing linearity. At the next stage we postulate facetwise proportionality or linearity as the case may be.

We can show how the introduction of linearity already enables some extension of our traditional results. Assume two sectors, manufacturing and social overhead capital. Social overhead capital enjoys increasing returns to scale so that input-output ratio falls as output expands. Then we have:

$$X_1 = a_{11}X_1 + a_{12}X_2 - \bar{a}_{12} + F_1$$
$$X_2 = a_{21}X_1 + a_{22}X_2 - \bar{a}_{22} + F_2$$

Then $\{X\} = [A]\{X\} + \{F - \bar{a}\}$ where $\{X\}$ is the column vector of gross output levels. $[A]$ is a matrix of marginal input-output coefficients. $\{F - \bar{a}\}$ stands for adjusted final demand.

Then, $\{X\} = [I - A]^{-1}\{F - \bar{a}\}$.

This differs from the traditional estimates of $\{X\}$ for any given amounts of $\{F\}$ by a factor $[I - A]^{-1}\{\bar{a}\}$ which may be sizeable depending on $\{\bar{a}\}$.

We may also introduce some inequalities such as for values $X < \bar{X}$, $X_{1j} = a_{1j} X_j$, but for values $> \bar{X}$, $X_{1j} = a_{1j}X_j$. This is what we mean by proportionality in facets. Even here we had best postulate proportionality in facets (stages) rather than continuous variability. This implies that at any point of time there is a proportional relationship between each input and output, although the coefficient of proportionality need not be the same as on any earlier occasion. Such piecewise variation of the coefficients is not quite easy to handle explicitly. Since the prices are changing between the various nodal points, the procedure of numerical extrapolation in this case must distinguish explicitly between *value* variables and *volume* variables. This raises the familiar problems of index number construction,

[1] H. B. Chenery, 'Patterns of Industrial Growth'. (Paper presented at the Washington Meeting of the Econometric Society, December 1959.)

which render such concepts as real income and investment somewhat ambiguous.

If, however, we are interested only in numerical extrapolation, not in an explicit solution, all that we need to do is to work on a set of fixed coefficients for one well-defined facet. Beyond that, a different set of coefficients will be needed, and the procedure may be repeated. This sounds slightly artificial because in reality the facets are not that precisely marked, but the advantage in the handling of the problem is very great on this assumption.

Another way of handling this problem of piecewise linearity may be to assume that substitutability operates only on *the margin*; that is to say, we may assume that the increment of capital stock may be used in various ratios with complementary factors, while once a choice has been made, we have a certain unique ratio in which the factors must be employed. Thus we have layers of capital stock and corresponding layers of technique and the relative importance of a given type of technique decreases in proportion as the importance of the corresponding layer of capital stock becomes less important. This comes about in two ways:

1. The capital stock of a special type depreciates.
2. It is not replaced by an old type but one appropriate to the changed conditions of the system.

This second approach is very interesting from the theoretical point of view, and it may be shown to be quite consistent with the first point of view, although computational problems suggested by its approach are not quite simple. Two things must be noted about the method of piecewise linearity:

First, at each point of time we must ascertain whether the conditions relating to the consistency of the various coefficients are satisfied. In case these coefficients turn out to be inconsistent, i.e. the Hawkins-Simons conditions of the system are not satisfied, this is presumably because the system determining the coefficients has more equations than unknowns. This *over-determination* arises because changes in the coefficient in one industry may well entail certain changes in other sets of co-efficients, which may not be immediately apparent. Thus by postulating constancy somewhere we are dealing with a structure implicitly over-determined. The reason why such over-

45

determination will not arise in this approach is that we allow for induced changes in the coefficients in a piecewise manner via the price effects.

Second, if the coefficients are changing as output increases, of course relative prices will be changing, which raises all the familiar index number difficulties in determining real income over time. Since index number problems are theoretically 'insoluble', we may have to ascertain *limits* within which such discrepancies will lie and then proceed as we would have done otherwise. A practical resolution of this difficulty may be indicated along the lines of successive iteration. This means that we plan for the sub-period for which prices are more or less constant, having sufficient regard for the terminal capital equipment. Then we repeat the procedure for the next sub-period, having regard for the terminal equipment at the end of this period. In this way we can avoid some of the difficulties in practice. This is of course analogous to the procedure on which chain indexes are constructed.

The last point relates to the way depreciation should be calculated. With straightline depreciation, 'depreciation' (amortization) exceeds 'replacement' in a growing economy, but in the context of numerical extrapolation there is no reason why we should use straightline depreciation. We may calculate 'depreciation' in such a way that the difference between depreciation and replacement does not exist. Where we are concerned more with 'real' conditions rather than with financial practices, such a procedure should not evoke much criticism.

APPENDIX

The Technique of Numerical Extrapolation

The technique of numerical extrapolation may be illustrated in the following way:

(*a*) Specify the initial condition:
For simplicity, we assume both the lags to be the same, i.e. $l_1 = l_2 = 3$. Then the number of arbitrary initial conditions equals 6. These are $K_1(0)$, $K_1(1)$, $K_1(2)$, and $K_2(0)$, $K_2(1)$, $K_2(2)$.

(*b*) The data of the system are: $[a_{1j}]$, $\{b\}$, $\{d\}$, s $[g]$

(c) The unknowns of the problem are: $K_1(3)$, $K_1(4)$, $K_1(5)$, and $K_2(3)$, $K_2(4)$, $K_2(5)$. They may be determined from our set of equations. Thus $K(3)$, $K(4)$, $K(5)$ are determined. In the second round, the data are the unknowns of the first stage, the constants may or may not remain unchanged, and the whole procedure will be repeated. Thus all the successive points in time will be reached, and the time path of all the variables will be ascertained in a stepwise fashion.

In the above example lags have been assumed to be the same in both the sectors. The more general situation, involving different gestation lags, may also be considered without introducing any difficulties.

4

THE USE OF SHADOW PRICES
IN PROGRAMME EVALUATION[1]

S. CHAKRAVARTY

I. INTRODUCTION

Some recent works on problems of economic development have emphasized one important proposition, i.e. that in under-developed countries one should use 'shadow prices' of productive factors rather than their observed market prices in determining the priorities in an investment programme.[2] By an investment programme we mean a design for determining an optimal product mix as well as an optimal technology for the productive sectors.

It is the purpose of this paper to discuss critically a range of issues connected with the use of shadow prices in programme evaluation. The issues are the following:

(a) What exactly we mean by shadow prices.

(b) The problem of estimating shadow prices of the relevant productive factors.

(c) If there exist ways of determining them approximately even though an exact solution may be out of reach.

(d) What the conditions are under which shadow prices would enable an optimal assignment of priorities.

(e) And finally to examine if there are situations where, although shadow prices do not lead in general to a proper assignment of priorities, yet within the context of an over-all optimal programme determined directly, they

---

[1] I am greatly indebted to Professor P. N. Rosenstein-Rodan for the suggestion of the problem and his stimulating comments. I am also very grateful to Professors R. M. Solow, R. S. Eckaus and I. M. D. Little and Mr Anisur Rahman for several penetrating discussions. None of them should, however, be held responsible for any of the views expressed here.

[2] J. Tinbergen, *The Design of Development* (Baltimore, Johns Hopkins Press, 1958); H. B. Chenery and P. G. Clark, *Interindustry Economics* (New York, John Wiley, 1959); H. B. Chenery, 'Development Policies and Programmes', *Economic Bulletin for Latin America*, III, No. 1 (March 1958).

may still be used to choose between relevant alternatives within somewhat narrower specifications. To mention a conclusion reached much later in discussion, it would be noticed that in the more realistic situation with which we are likely to be faced, it is only an affirmative answer to question (*e*) which assigns a proper measure of importance to shadow prices in programme evaluation.

So far as the estimation problems are concerned, we shall illustrate our argument with reference to the shadow prices of capital and foreign exchange, which figure in common discussion as two of the most important productive factors in the context of planning in underdeveloped areas. It may be thought a little surprising to use capital and foreign exchange as two separate factors since our usual definition of a factor of production runs in terms of a group of productive agents which have a very high elasticity of substitution among themselves, but between which and other productive agents the elasticity of substitution is zero or nearly zero. On this basis it may be questioned if capital and foreign exchange are such imperfect substitutes for each other as to be described as separate factors. It must be conceded that there is nothing *a priori* about this division. It is based on the assumption, a very realistic one for many underdeveloped countries, that possibilities of exporting and importing commodities at roughly unchanged prices are *extremely low* or, roughly, non-existent. This means that substitution possibilities are so severely limited as to make it a convenient simplification to use them as separate factors.

II. THE CONCEPT AND RATIONALE OF SHADOW PRICES

In the language of programming, shadow prices are nothing but the Lagrange multipliers of a constrained optimization problem. An equivalent way of describing them is in terms of the optimal solution of the so-called symmetric 'dual' problem. Their plain economic meaning is none other than that of marginal value productivity of the productive factors in an optimal situation when all alternative uses have been taken into account. The reason why shadow prices are considered to be important for an economist is that neo-classical theory of resource allocation tells us that the value of the national product at given prices of final commodities is maximized if productive factors are employed so as to equate their value productivities with their rentals.

It so happens that the rules of the game associated with perfect competition also lead to an identical result, e.g. equivalence of marginal productivities with rentals. But the connection with institutional aspects of perfect competition in this context is incidental. What is important is the use of prices as parameters in deciding how much to produce. There are several reasons why observed prices in an underdeveloped economy deviate from prices as calculated from the optimizing solution of a programming problem: the institutional context of perfect competition is almost entirely absent; there are structural shortages which do not respond to price changes, which in some cases is not an unmixed evil from the wider sociological point of view, for example, where marginal productivity of labour is zero, and the corresponding shadow price of labour should also be zero, but the market has to assign a non-zero wage level to labour just to keep them alive; there is the problem that prices do not reflect and hence do not transmit all the direct and indirect influences on the cost as well as on the demand side, which under smoother conditions they would.

Now it should be obvious that if our objective is to maximize the value of national income, then prices which should be regarded as pointers in planning investment are not the market prices but what are called shadow prices.

There are, however, questions which may be raised at this stage: How do we know these shadow prices? And even if we know them from an optimal programme in the sense discussed above, they may not be the appropriate ones, because the interest of the planner may lie not in maximizing current national income but some other objective or a combination of objectives.

The second question, however, is in a sense not an important one, because the logic of using shadow prices is quite independent of the nature of the specific preference function that has been set up. Shadow prices in the programming interpretation are perfectly neutral with respect to the type of maximization that is employed; although their interpretation as prices which would be realized under perfect competition is not.

But there is a somewhat related question, though a different one, which is not purely semantic. This is concerned with the empirical proposition that planners suggest, and, given the power, carry out, certain types of investment which yield results over finite though long periods of time. In certain extreme cases these projects do not yield results at all for some time to come. In evaluating such projects, to take into account only the impact on current national income is not appropriate. But if future experiences are to count, shadow prices calculated as of contemporary scarcities would not be proper.

In planning for economic development the endowments of the relevant primary factors are continually changing and their scarcity aspects are therefore shifting. Hence, what we need for such purposes is not merely the shadow price relating to one point of time, but the development of shadow prices over a period of time, i.e. the time path of shadow prices. Without such an estimate of the time path, there may arise a systematic bias against the use of long-run projects if the shadow prices implied in maximizing current production were the only ones to be used.

Once, however, the values and time paths of these prices have been ascertained, there is no doubt they would greatly simplify the lack of assigning detailed priorities. Construction of adequate 'benefit-cost' ratios for the investment projects is possible on the basis of these estimates only. They could then be employed to discriminate among projects, in view of all the interdependences existing at a point of time as well as over a period of time.

Granted what has been said above, we have to turn to the first question, which is the crucial one: How do we know these proper shadow prices? If they are known, then the optimal pattern of capital accumulation is already known, and vice versa. Thus we are not offering the planners anything immediately practical when we advise them to solve a problem in dynamic programming, however simplified its structure may be.[1]

At this stage the argument for shadow prices rests on our ability to devise certain approximations which do not require

[1] S. Chakravarty, 'An Outline of a Method for Programme Evaluation' (this volume, pp. 33-47); R. Dorfman, P. A. Samuelson and R. Solow, *Linear Programming and Economic Analysis* (New York, McGraw-Hill, 1958).

the solution of a full-scale dynamic programming problem. Thus we may first solve a programming model on a relatively very high degree of aggregation and determine the time path of prices of important groups of productive factors such as labour, capital, and foreign exchange. Having attained these broad estimates, we may be justified in using them for purposes of assigning detailed priorities to the investment projects in various sectors.

Thus the derivation of shadow prices on a more aggregative and hence approximate basis, together with the decision rule to maximize net incomes or net discounted value of earnings at these prices, would already go a long way to devising more efficient methods of programme evaluation.

An even more approximate procedure would be to use some general qualitative features of capital accumulation in an economy whose structural characteristics are well known to make certain approximate estimates of ranges within which shadow prices of important productive factors might be expected to lie. This is attempted in our discussion of shadow rate of interest on the basis of the qualitative characteristics of a multi-sector growth process. Discussion on this point is meant only to suggest certain limits without pretending at quantitative exactitude.

Since the present practice in development programming is based almost exclusively on the current market prices of primary factors which are heavily out of line with their 'intrinsic' values, even the use of such approximate shadow prices would lead to a more efficient resource allocation, provided the estimates are correct in a qualitative sense.

III. THE PROBLEM OF ESTIMATION

The Shadow Price of Foreign Exchange
It is a well-known observation that the shadow price of foreign exchange in many underdeveloped countries suffering from chronic balance of payments difficulties is substantially higher than the official rate of exchange. The reason for such maintained prices of foreign currency is that, price elasticity of the exports and imports being quite low, the mechanism of letting price find its own level by equating the total demand for foreign

currency to the total supply of foreign currency either does not work or works at the expense of income growth. Further, there is a widespread opinion that balance of payments difficulties of newly developing countries are transitional in character, so that once certain structural changes have been well under way, excessive demand for imports or diversion of exports to home uses may cease, thus making it possible to approximate closely the equilibrium rate of exchange.[1]

Thus while it is necessary to maintain an official rate of exchange different from the shadow rate, the shadow rate will still be the appropriate one to use in order to *discriminate* between alternative programmes or, in marginal cases, between alternative projects. Since sectors as well as the processes within any sector differ remarkably with respect to foreign exchange requirements, direct and cumulative, such discrimination is essential in order to satisfy the constraint relating to balance of payments equilibrium. If these constraints refer to different points of time, a time path of the shadow rate of exchange will be involved rather than a single rate of exchange to be applied indefinitely. The standard procedure to determine the shadow rate of exchange at a point of time is to solve a programming problem of the following type:

Maximize a certain preference function, e.g. value of national income, subject to a specification of technology and a prescribed level of primary factors, including foreign exchange availability.[2] Such models have been extensively studied by Chenery, who normally expresses the preference function in terms of minimizing capital needed subject to final demand restriction, technology, and foreign exchange earnings. Chenery also includes import substitution as a built-in choice problem even

[1] One may argue for a devaluation of the home currency instead of letting the exchange rate seek its own level. This, however, runs into problems that are not entirely economic in character. Further, too frequent devaluations, depending on the variations in the import composition of the successive plans, will introduce nearly the same type of destabilizing influence as the method of floating exchange rates.

[2] The more general approach including balance of payments deficit (or surplus), as well as the rate of growth of income in the social welfare function, cannot be implemented unless we have some method of numerically estimating the relative rates of substitution among the different policy objectives. No very convenient method exists in this connection, notwithstanding the contribution of Frisch. R. Frisch, 'The Numerical Determination of the Coefficients of a Preference Function' (Norway, University of Oslo). (Mimeographed.)

when alternative techniques are ruled out. When exports are not infinitely elastic, we have a problem in non-linear programming which has also been considered by him.[1] In keeping with what has been said in I, if the type of problem considered by Chenery in its static aspects is extended to take into account interdependences in time, in the form of usual recursion relationships that characterize a dynamic model, then the corresponding preference function can be expressed in a large number of ways. Some details along these lines have been investigated in a somewhat different context.[2]

But the upshot of the whole thing is to pose a problem having significant dimensions, although part of the dimension difficulties may be reduced by taking advantage of block-triangularity, characterizing dynamic Leontief-type models. The way out of these difficulties from the computational point of view is as follows.

Develop a programming model, linear or non-linear, which emphasizes heavily the sectors which engage in international trade either through earning foreign exchange or through consuming foreign exchange on a significant scale. Aggregate the remaining sectors considerably. Solve the resulting maximization problem and then compute the shadow rate of exchange from this approximate analysis. This preserves a certain notion of optimization, which we associate with shadow prices of primary factors.

The alternative to this procedure is to compute the demand for and supply of foreign exchange and then determine the rate which equilibrates the two. We should be clear that since equilibrium is attainable at many different levels of income, there is no guarantee that this equilibrium rate of exchange is the same as the shadow rate of exchange defined in the preceding paragraphs. However, such an estimate may be useful to know as summarizing all the relevant information involved in a development plan bearing on the foreign exchange situation. This computation may be done on a very aggregative level, as well as on relatively disaggregated levels. Naturally, the

---

[1] H. B. Chenery and H. Uzawa, 'Non-Linear Programming in Economic Development', *Studies in Linear and Non-Linear Programming*, edited by K. J. Arrow, L. Hurwicz and H. Uzawa (Stanford, Stanford University Press, 1958).

[2] Dorfman, Samuelson and Solow, *op. cit.*, Chapter 12.

accuracy of the estimates would improve, depending on how detailed the data happen to be.

The following notations are employed in the formula for determining the shadow rate of exchange:

$\{e\}$ — Column vector of exports.

$\{e'\}$ — is the corresponding row vector.

$\{w\}$ — Column vector of investment delivered by the sectors.

$\{w\}$ — Column vector of investment received by the sectors.

$\{c\}$ — Column vector of final consumption.

$\bar{p}$ — Price level of goods produced at home.

$\{p\}$ — Vector of domestic prices.

$\{p_m\}$ — Price of imports, here assumed to be homogeneous for simplicity.

k — The shadow rate of exchange.

m_1 — The quantity of raw materials imported.

m_2 — The quantity of investment goods imported.

m_3 — Import of consumer goods.

Coefficients:

$\{a\}$ — Leontief's matrix of flow coefficients.

$\{v_1\}$ — Row vector of imports per unit of gross output. These may also be called noncompetitive import requirements per unit of output.

$\{v_2\}$ — Row vector of imports per unit of investment received. This gives the import composition of the investment programme.

v_3 — The functional dependence of imports of consumer goods on home consumption and the relative prices at home and abroad.

M — Total value of imports (measured in domestic prices).

E — Total value of exports (measured in domestic prices).

D — Permissible balance of payments deficit. This need not be a single number, but may only indicate a range within which the deficits should lie.

The problem then consists in determining the value or values of 'k' so that the balance of payments deficits are confined to a certain preassigned range determined by *possibilities regarding foreign aid*. Since the estimates are seldom precise, it is useful to work out alternative values of 'k' corresponding to a whole range of possibilities relating to 'D'. In principle we can solve the various numerical situations to get a step-function relating the shadow rate of exchange to the parameter 'D' assumed variable over a certain range. Assuming, however, that the plan specifies a set of values of {e}, {w}, and {c}, and the coefficients are inflexible, then 'k' is the only variable to adapt itself to such predetermined magnitudes. It will, however, be desirable to determine the *sensitivity of 'k' to adjustment in some of the physical magnitudes* which are subject to some degree of control, e.g. {w}, which gives the import composition of investment, or {c}, the import of consumer goods. We have the following final equation for this purpose:

$$\overline{D}=M-E$$
$$=kp_m m-e'p$$
$$=kp_m(m_1+m_2+m_3)-e'p$$
$$\overline{D}=kp_m\{\,\{v_1\}(I-a)^{-1}(e+w+c)+v_2\{\overline{w}\}+v_3(c,\overline{p}-p_m)\}$$
$$-\{p_1e_1+p_2e_2+\ldots+p_ne_n\}$$

We give 'n' export quantities for generality, but some of these will be identically equal to zero since we have sectors, for example, services, which do not export anything. The dimensionalities in matrix multiplication are also properly observed in as much as $\{v_1\}$ is $(1\times n)$, $(I-a)^{-1}$ is $(n\times n)$, $(e+w+c)$ is $(n\times 1)$. Thus the whole expression is (1×1) and may be multiplied by 'p_m' to get the value in foreign currency of the required amount of imports of raw materials.

$\{\overline{w}\}$ and $\{w\}$ are connected by the following matrix equation: $\{w\}=[w]\{\overline{w}\}$ where $[w]$ is the matrix of investment coefficients.[1]

Each 'p_n' may be written in the following way: (2) $p_i = A_{oi}kp_m+$other terms $i=1\ldots n$. The other terms indicate the influence of whatever other primary factors are assumed to be important. Thus we have $(n+1)$ equations to determine the $(n+1)$ unknowns, the shadow rate of exchange, 'k' and 'n'

[1] For a discussion of this matrix, see the author's *The Logic of Investment Planning* (Amsterdam, North Holland Publishing Company, 1959), Chapter V.

domestic prices. This circularity arises because the production of domestic goods needs imports, and as such prices of domestic goods are dependent on prices of imports as expressed in domestic currency.

The above analysis may be easily extended to take into account the heterogeneity of imports, and thus we need not assume only one composite type of imports which is capable of being used for various functional purposes. (The extension is of merely algebraic nature and may be easily worked out.)

It should be apparent from the above discussion that exports for this purpose have been assumed to be exogenously prescribed. This is a simplification, although of a nature that is not *difficult to justify*, especially when price *elasticity of exports is very low or low in relation to the other factors involved*. These other factors involve both the level of world demand as determined by rising world incomes and the domestic expansion of demand for export commodities. If the price elasticities are assumed to be significant, then this may also be taken account of by a further complication in analysis. But then, to retain manageability, we should have to restrict the number of sectors very considerably.

The Shadow Rate of Interest
The shadow rate of interest is commonly regarded as a concept more difficult than the shadow rate of foreign exchange. One reason for this is that in the case of foreign exchange we are concerned exclusively with flow magnitudes, so much imports representing a flow demand for foreign currency and so much exports representing a flow supply of foreign currency. The shadow rate of exchange equilibrates the demand and supply of foreign currency. With the shadow rate of interest, however, we are concerned with relations between stock and flow, and a very large variety of stocks at that. Further, these stocks have different degrees of durability. Thus it becomes extremely complicated if we want to get one single measure of these stocks, as we normally do in talking about 'the amount of capital' and 'the rate of interest'.

The presence of double index number ambiguity, one due to cross-sectional aspects and the other due to longitudinal or intertemporal aspects of capital, makes the interpretation of

57

this single measure somewhat dubious. Nonetheless, it has heuristic significance, as more rigorous models involving multiple capital goods seem to indicate.[1] The logically rigorous way of deriving these interest rates, one for each stock, which under certain circumstances equal each other, is to specify the decision problem as one in dynamic programming, with appropriate initial and boundary conditions. Choice of natural boundary conditions is not an easy question. For absence of 'compactness' in the policy space, infinity does not serve as a proper boundary condition in most economic problems extending over time.[2]

All these theoretical considerations are, however, poor consolation for the planner if the policy-maker is concerned with rationing out scarce capital amongst a number of competing projects. True enough that if we know the solution to a full-fledged dynamic programming problem, we know at the same time the shadow rates of interest, because the *optimum programme of capital accumulation determines the shadow rates of interest.* In that context they may be used to decentralize decision-making by permitting simple decision rules to be specified. But when that is not feasible, we still need a kind of *computational shorthand in order to rank projects.* Whatever approximations we may devise for computing the shadow rate of interest, even though they are correct in only a qualitative sense, will be more useful than relying on the observed market rate of interest in economies characterized by market imperfections, etc.

In the subsequent paragraphs, certain considerations relating to the shadow rate of interest are discussed under the following sets of assumptions.

(*A*) Where *capital stocks* are growing at the same proportionate rate and the production functions are linear and homogeneous;

(*B*) Where the relative rates of growth of the capital stocks

---

[1] P. A. Samuelson and R. M. Solow, 'A Complete Capital Model Involving Heterogeneous Capital Goods', *Quarterly Journal of Economics*, Vol. 70, November 1956.

[2] For a discussion of this point see the author's 'On the Existence of an Optimum Savings Program' (Cambridge, Mass., Center for International Studies, M.I.T., 1960). (Mimeographed.)

are different, but we still maintain the linear homogeneity assumption;

(C) Where the production functions are no longer assumed to satisfy the linear homogeneity conditions, and the equiproportionate rate of growth of all the sector does not hold.

We shall discuss these various cases in the order presented above.

(A) This situation may be further subdivided into the following two cases: (i) where there is no final demand, and (ii) where the system admits of final demand, i.e. not all the net product is reinvested. An illustration of case (i) is the closed dynamic model enunciated by Von Neumann in the early thirties. The specific setup of the Von Neumann model is well known and does not require any repetition. Von Neumann stated as the main conclusion of his investigation the now famous equality between the rate of interest and the maximum rate of balanced growth that the system can perform. The maximum rate of balanced growth is known to satisfy the criterion of inter-temporal efficiency. But as such, it is one among an infinite number of efficient paths. Solow and Samuelson have shown that for situations referring to sufficiently distant points of time, and preference function involving terminal stocks of different commodities, the maximal rate of steady growth is the best way in which the system may be allowed to grow, excepting for a finite number of time periods. The length of the period for which the system is allowed to deviate from the Von Neumann model of growth is independent of the time horizon. Admittedly, this is true for 'closed systems', e.g. systems admitting no autonomous consumption. But as a first approximation for economies on a very low level of real income, a closed model, particularly one such as Von Neumann's, which allows for different patterns of consumption in the same way that it includes different techniques for producing a particular commodity, it may not be entirely dismissed out of hand. Hence the above consideration is not entirely irrelevant from the empirical viewpoint, although from the purely logical point of view its special nature should be clearly understood.

The Von Neumann model of a closed expanding economy has been generalized by Solow and Malinvaud, who relax the assumption that all the net product is reinvested. In other words, they assume the savings coefficient to be less than unity. Despite differences in presentation, the relationship between the rate of interest and the rate of growth given by the above authors is the same.

The following expression of the relationship is due to Solow[1] who considers both the capitalists and the wage earners to be saving constant proportions of their incomes:

$$\rho = \frac{g}{\sigma_R + \dfrac{1-D}{D}\sigma_w}$$

where: ρ is the rate of interest

g is the rate of growth

σ_R is the savings coefficient for profit receivers

σ_w is the savings coefficient for wage earners

D is the share of profit incomes in total income

It is evident that the $\rho \gtreqless g$ according as the denominator is ≤ 1. Now the denominator may be written as follows:

$$\frac{D\sigma_R + (1-D)\sigma_w}{D}$$

The expression $D\sigma_R + (1-D)\sigma_w$ is nothing other than the weighted average of the two savings coefficients or the savings coefficient for the economy as a whole. Thus we may write

$\rho = \dfrac{g}{s/D}$ where 's' is the global savings ratio. That this relation-

ship is merely a generalization of the Von Neumann result may be seen easily. On the specific Von Neumann assumption that $\sigma_R = 1$ and $\sigma_w = 0$, the above formula indicates $\rho = g$. When σ_w is allowed to assume positive values, there are other constellations of the coefficients for which equality holds. Although the formula indicates the theoretical possibility that the rate of interest may be lower than the rate of growth, whatever empirical evidence we have rules out this as a realistic case. Thus we may be justified to consider the equality as the limiting case.

[1] R. M. Solow, 'Notes Towards a Wicksellian Theory of Distributive Share' (Cambridge, Mass., Department of Economics, M.I.T., 1961). (Mimeographed.)

From the data given by S. J. Patel,[1] it appears that 's/D' in India may lie somewhere between ·5 and ·3 depending on how one classifies income in the household sectors. Thus, if we assume a maximal rate of steady growth of income at 4 per cent, the rate of interest lies between 8 per cent and 12 per cent. It is obvious that with a larger rate of growth the equilibrium value of the rate of interest goes up, and with a higher rate of savings it falls.

The use of the above formula may enable us to calculate limits for the shadow rate of interest if our *a priori* knowledge strongly indicates that the 'real scarcity' of capital is greater than would be indicated by the currently ruling rate of interest. In that case the limits are given by the current rate, on the one hand, and by the formula connecting the rate of interest with the maximal rate of steady growth on the other. The maximal rate of steady growth may be calculated on a first approximation from the set of data usually given in the two Leontief matrices. With the Leontief assumptions the maximal rate of steady growth is determined by the Frobenius root of the matrix $B (I-A)^{-1}$, which is naturally non-negative. For more general situations, the computational difficulties would be much greater.[2]

There are two points that one should remember in this context:

1. The rate of interest as calculated on the above approach is not 'the rate of interest' as usually understood in connection with the capital or money market. This should be obvious, because the model does not introduce uncertainty and corresponding distinction between various types of assets.

2. The rate of interest as deduced from the Solow formula is different from the pure rate of time discount. It takes into account both productivity and thrift. The influence of productivity is taken into account in the numerator, while the savings coefficient subsumes the influence of thrift. Behind thrift lies the factor of time preference. The rate of pure time discount

---

[1] *Indian Economic Review*, February 1956.

[2] In using the formula for the generalized Von Neumann situation we should consider whether the decision on the savings rate is an optimal one or not. If no optimality considerations may be adduced for the savings coefficient, the rate of interest calculated from the Solow expression would not measure the intrinsic scarcity of capital.

that is involved may be estimated if we assume that the observed savings rate is the result of an operational decision to maximize the sum of discounted values of consumption over a period of time. This is similar to the famous Ramsey model of optimal savings. The difference consists in introducing a non-zero rate of time discount which Ramsey would have found ethically inappropriate, and in the further restriction that is involved in reducing the 'path maximum' problem to a 'point maximum' problem. By a 'point maximum' problem we mean the problem of maximizing an integral of discounted utilities, by a once-for-all choice of savings rate. The period of time may be finite or infinite, depending on the planner's point of view. In the finite case there should be a provision for terminal equipment. Then for every savings rate we can find the underlying rate of time preference.

This problem has been investigated by Tinbergen.[1] He gives a number of equilibrium relations involving the rate of time discount, the savings rate, and the capital coefficient each based on a specific hypothesis relating to the utility function. The utility function underlying the simplest problem is in his case a logarithmic one. It should, however, be noted that our problem here is the logical inverse to Tinbergen's problem. He is interested in finding out the optimum rate of savings corresponding to any given values of the capital-coefficient, and time preference. In our case, we want to know the underlying time preference, assuming that the savings rate is already an optimal one, other parameters remaining the same.

The Tinbergen result can be generalized by introducing more general types of production functions and utility functions other than the logarithmic or hyperbolic ones considered by him. There is scope for much further investigations along these lines.

(B) We now consider the situation when all the sectors are not assumed to grow at the same proportionate rate, but all the relevant production functions have the needed convexity properties.

In this case the relative prices and the interest rate are no longer constant. Since the rate of growth is not a unique number characterizing the entire process, we have to deal with the

[1] J. Tinbergen, 'The Optimum Rate of Savings', *The Economic Journal*, Vol. LXVI, December 1956.

constantly changing moving equilibria, as it were, and the relation in which the growth rate stands to the rate of interest would therefore be continually shifting. Further, 'the growth rate' in this case is itself a somewhat ambiguous concept. Also, the various own rates of interest do not any longer equal the own rate of interest for the numeraire commodity. It therefore inescapably appears that we could say very little on the question without going the whole hog of solving a problem in dynamic programming. In principle, an optimal solution is always possible in case (*B*) but to reach it we have to specify first the appropriate terminal conditions, the initial stocks, and the time profile of consumption over the entire period. Having done that, we have to apply the usual techniques of maximization over time.[1]

IV. THE CALCULATION OF PRIORITIES

In this section we consider the method of calculating priorities in an investment programme by using shadow prices. We must bear in mind that while we calculate the benefit-cost ratios for a single project, we do it as of a given programme and not for the project in isolation. This follows from the fact that the projects are necessarily interlinked and imply certain assumptions about the rest of the economy. Thus one project may be chosen from a set of competing projects if the rest of the programmes may be assumed to be relatively unaffected by this choice.

We may also consider a more generalized situation where there is a technically nonseparable collection of projects which can be singled out for piecemeal decision-making. Now in this case this whole collection has to be treated as one unit, and the benefit-cost calculations have to be calculated for this one unit as a whole. The words 'technical nonseparability' are important in this connection. The assumption of linear homogeneity is crucial to the applicability of the shadowprice argument as usually understood. This is because the logic of applying shadow prices is in essence an argument for piecemeal decision-making. Piecemeal decision-making in situations characterized by increasing returns or significant external economies either leads

---

[1] Such problems have been considered in the preceding paper. For a general reference see Dorfman, Samuelson and Solow, *loc. cit.*

to insufficient output or to no production at all. This causes difficulties with respect to the remainder of the programme where the outputs of the above sectors serve as technologically necessary ingredients. Thus it appears that in these situations the better procedure is to solve the entire problem simultaneously as as an example of co-ordinated decision-making.[1]

The advantage of the shadow price technique becomes considerably greater if the complex of planning problems may be assumed to be decomposable into the following stages:

(a) How much to invest in total over a number of years,

(b) How to distribute the total investment resources among different sectors of the economy,

(c) How to choose the best method of utilizing the resources allocated to a sector.

If the stages are strictly consecutive we may think that the decision on level (b) is reached on the basis of maximizing income over a period of time subject to all the interdependencies in production, investment and consumption. This would roughly indicate how much to invest in each sector. If there are sectors like social overhead capital where investment is made on grounds independent of any maximization process, then we should consider the remaining sub-set of sectors for our decision purposes.

The decision on stage (c) can be reached on the basis of utilizing a shadow rate of interest and for a given time profile of production on the requirement that the costs are minimized.

In theory as well as practice, the stages may not be that distinct, in which case decisions on (b) and (c) may have to be reached simultaneously. The shadow rate technique should then be replaced by the general methods of dynamic programming.

Now let us consider the problem quantitatively. We use the following notations:

$W_1(t)$ — The investment in the project per unit time.

---

[1] Possibilities of decentralized decision-making in situations characterized by the absence of classical homogeneity or independence assumption have been investigated in the important paper by K. J. Arrow and L. Hurwicz, 'Decentralization and Computation in Resource Allocation', *Essays in Economics and Econometrics; a Volume in Honour of Harold Hotelling*, edited by R. W. Pfouts (Chapel Hill, University of North Carolina Press, 1960).

$F_1(t)$ — The foreign component of investment per unit time.

$F_1 = aW_1$ where $0 \le a \le 1$.

g — The length of the gestation period.

n — The length of the operating period.

r — The shadow rate of interest.

k — The shadow rate of exchange.

$D(t)$ — The current operating expenses of a project.

Then the cost of a project may be calculated as follows:

We have $F_1 = aW_1$

Therefore $H_1 = (1-a)W_1$ where H_1 is the domestic component of investment. Since we value the foreign investment component at the shadow exchange rate, we have:

$$kaW_1 + (1-a)W_1 = W_1(ka + 1 - a)$$
$$= W_1\{1 - a(1-k)\}$$

Let us assume that we know the timeshape on construction effort: $W(t)$. Then the cost of investment in the project may be calculated as:

$$C = \overset{o}{\underset{t=g}{\Sigma}} W(t)\{1 - a(1-k)\}(1+r)^{-t} + \overset{n}{\underset{o}{\Sigma}} D(t)(1+r)^{-t}$$

The first term on the left-hand side indicates the investment that is made during the gestation period of the project and the second part indicates the cost that is incurred during the exploitation period. The decision rule consists in minimizing 'C' for a given time profile of 'output'. To put it differently, the projects to be compared are those which give the same time profile of output as that given by the over-all planning problem. Out of these projects, the one will be chosen which minimizes total cost over the combined gestation and exploitation period of the project.

V. CONCLUSION

Briefly stated, our discussion has clearly indicated that the technique of using shadow prices serves as a useful computational shorthand in devising a relatively 'efficient' system of programme evaluation. The qualification on 'efficiency' arises because in the presence of non-convexities in the production

E

processes of certain sectors the shadow price device does not enable one to reach the 'efficient' constellation of the system. The advantage from using shadow prices holds good even though the shadow prices we use are not exact but merely approximations, although it is important that they should be in the right direction. Given the data, the calculation of the shadow rate of exchange does not raise great difficulties. The simplified procedure indicated in this paper, or the more elaborate linear programming method discussed by Chenery, may be usefully employed. With respect to the shadow rate of interest, the conceptual difficulties are greater. But if we use the approximation procedure outlined earlier in this paper, we get a range of 8 per cent to 12 per cent for the shadow rate of interest under Indian conditions. The exact shadow rate of interest may be higher than this, but it is unlikely that this would be lower than given by this range. This already gives us a basis for judging projects which are economic only if the rate of interest is 4 per cent or $4\frac{1}{2}$ per cent.

The relevance of the shadow prices to practical problems may be understood if we take into account the problem of choosing between importing fertilizer or importing machinery for a fertilizer plant, or importing machinery for manufacturing fertilizer producing equipment. In the simple Austrian models, where choice is confined to a pair of alternatives, the cost of one is the opportunity foregone with the other projects. This is difficult to apply if there exists a manifold of possibilities for each unit of investment. Under such conditions the opportunity cost of a unit of investment is measured by its shadow rate of interest. Similarly, the cost of a unit of import should be valued at the shadow rate of exchange rather than at the official rate. If we take, for example, a shadow rate of exchange of Rs. 6 to a dollar and a rate of interest lying between 8 per cent and 12 per cent, we may calculate the cost of each type of project over the gestation period, given the time shape of the construction effort. Further, with a given time profile of output, in this case agricultural production, we can calculate the total costs for each project, e.g. investment costs and operating costs. Naturally, with other things remaining the same, the project with the lowest cost should be chosen.

The same line of reasoning may be applied to other problems

such as the choice between various types of power stations. An interesting contribution in this regard is the paper of Professor P. N. Rosenstein-Rodan on the contribution of atomic energy to India's development programme.

All this is to suggest the fruitfulness of the shadow price method in practical policy making if appropriate qualifications are borne in mind.

5

CHOICE ELEMENTS
IN INTERTEMPORAL PLANNING[1]

S. CHAKRAVARTY

R. S. ECKAUS

The utility of intertemporal or dynamic planning arises not only from its formulation of future goals but also from its specification of the means to achieve those goals. A plan for economic development is not just a set of targets. To be operational it must specify the measures necessary to achieve those targets.

An intertemporal plan is like a guide map. It shows the beginning and ending of the journey and the road to be travelled in order to make the trip. Just as incomplete maps would result in wasted effort, in the same way, short-term or annual plans are by themselves inadequate planning tools. The increasing uncertainty of longer periods, the inevitable short-run deviations from prescribed paths, the changes in technological possibilities, for example—all such influences justify annual and short-term plans. But such plans will be most effective when placed in the context of a long-term plan with its broader perspective and greater flexibility. Only long-term plans moreover can adequately encompass projects with long technical gestation periods and other slowly working initiatives.

The same type of influences which justify short-term plans necessitate frequent replanning on a long-term basis. This means that long-term planning, like short-term planning, is not a once-and-for-all operation. It must be a continuing process with modifications in the light of new knowledge and changing objectives and for elaboration to greater detail.

All planning is a political as well as an economic process. Though the political constraints often remain implicit in an economic programme, they constitute the boundaries within

---

[1] The authors acknowledge the helpful comments of Messrs Andreatta, Harberger and Sevaldson while retaining full responsibility for any errors.

which the economist must work. The components of economic policy are often competing, however, as regards both means and choice of ends; and the difficulties in political decisions arise not so much in formulating the ideals of a good life as in making the inevitable choices among its components. The economist therefore has the responsibility of defining the economic content of the political constraints given to him and to demonstrate the implications of alternative policies for concrete economic magnitudes.

I. THE CHOICE ELEMENTS IN INTERTEMPORAL PLANNING

In plans as in life not every wish can be satisfied and not every element can be chosen independently. There are political constraints which we shall not attempt to explore in detail here and economic constraints which we shall illustrate. These constraints arise out of the economic structure and the inter-relationships within it. In any planning model there must be a number of options which can be utilized to achieve a pre-ferred economic situation. We refer to these options as choice elements in the planning problem. The precise nature of these choice elements and the manner in which they may be deter-mined depend on the way the planning problem is posed and the type of planning model which is set up. In a planning model whose purpose is simply consistency, i.e. the determination of an intertemporal path of resource allocations and output levels which will lead from a given initial position to a specified ter-minal stock, there are four such choice elements: (1) the initial level of consumption, (2) the planning horizon, (3) the growth of consumption during the plan period, (4) the terminal condi-tions. Not all of these can be chosen independently. Once three are stipulated, the feasibility, and in that case the magnitude, of the fourth are also determined.[1] However, for planning models whose purpose is to determine the 'best' of all possible paths of development which connects two different positions in time these choice elements will have to be reformulated.

[1] In the implementation of a plan there will be many more detailed choices to be made such as the relative emphasis to be given to import-saving or export-gaining industries and the choice of the technologies which will be used. These choices, however, while of great significance, are derivative and constitute a choice of means rather than ends.

Since the concept of a 'best path' is itself a matter for discussion, we shall take up this reformulation in Section III of this chapter. In this section and the subsequent one we deal only with the first type, the consistency model.

1. *Levels of Consumption and Saving at the Beginning of a Plan*
The point need not be elaborated that most of the resources required for growth in any country must be provided internally. Just as the productive resources currently available depend on past accumulation, so also the endowment which the present leaves to the future depends on the manner in which current resources are allocated between consumption and investment.

The vicious circle of poverty and stagnation from which the less-developed countries are trying to escape sets limits on the proportion of output from currently available resources which can be diverted from consumption to building up productive resources for future use. The proportion can be changed, however, by individuals in some of the income brackets, at least, and by the state in pursuance of the national goals. This proportion is one of the fundamental choice elements in planning.

Most important from the viewpoint of planning is that the State can affect the initial levels of consumption and saving by the various tax and control measures at its command. The economic analysis of alternative policies should not obscure the fact that the choice is essentially political. In some countries physical coercion has been used. Where such means are abhorrent, fiscal and other indirect devices are employed and the element of state coercion becomes less obvious. These indirect measures are likely to have a limited scope where consumption is already low, but they are not without effect.

To force down consumption by any means will be a difficult process. More often the practical issue is to what level it will be allowed to rise. The decisions have to be political, but their consequences are profoundly economic. This also applies to the degree of inequality of consumption which is tolerated in the process of development. Inequality influences the level and pattern of consumption and may be as significant in the latter respect as in the former since the consumption of the upper-income groups makes special demands on such particularly scarce resources as foreign exchange. Therefore a redistribution of income, or of poverty, to put the point another way, may be required to create the initial conditions necessary to achieve the other economic goals which a nation sets for itself.

2. Time Horizon of Planning

The choice of a time horizon for planning is not just a question of whether there are technical-economic reasons for a five-year plan or a ten- or twenty-year plan, though these are important. Some of the most important projects require long periods to show their full benefits. In addition, the choice of a time horizon also influences the manner in which the sacrifices and benefits of economic growth should be distributed over time. The choice of a planning horizon of 50 years, for example, at the end of which relative austerity would be relaxed, would be one aspect of a decision to deny the present generation any of the fruits of its own labour and sacrifice. A planning horizon of five years may imply the opposite.

There are technical-economic reasons for a long-term plan rather than a short-term plan in the opportunities the former provides for foresight and continuity of effort. These reasons are not finally decisive. For example, a policy of preparation for imminent doomsday would override such arguments and dictate short-term planning in spite of its limitations.

The choice of the length of the planning horizon is more usually an implicit rather than an explicit decision in planning. Although this decision affects the path and content of economic growth in an essential, if intricate, way, the alternative choices are less fully debated than, say, questions related to current consumption and savings levels which may seem to be more tangible and pressing. The time horizon issues, however, have not been completely ignored. A common policy statement is that the present generation should participate in the benefits of the future economic growth for which it is making sacrifices. An explicit and open policy to the contrary has rarely if ever been enunciated in any country.

Yet the meaning of the policy of participation by the present generation in the returns for present sacrifices has to be spelled out. Today's patriarch cannot expect the same future benefits as the schoolboy. Still the impossibility of promising fully equal participation does not prevent establishment of some standards of equity. One such standard would be that a representative member of the current population should have a better future. Another slightly different criterion would set this goal for an average person in the present labour force. For the application of such criteria the average length of life is important or, more precisely, the average life expectancy of the population or of members of the labour force. For the present population of India as a whole the average life expectancy is in the neighbourhood of 32 years. It is substantially less for members of the current labour force. This suggests a limit to the postponement of the enjoyment of the fruits of development on the basis of either of the above standards of equity.

As the time horizon of planning is shifted further into the future, the main variables of an intertemporal planning model are significantly affected. Since results are so critically related to the choice of a single number which is bound to be somewhat arbitrary in character, economists have sometimes been tempted to set the planning horizon infinitely far off into the future. For certain types of analytical problems this particular choice of a boundary condition in time is useful. But, particularly in a consistency model, there would be something contradictory in postulating a set of finite terminal conditions to be reached only over an infinite period of time. This consideration is logically sufficient to rule infinity out of consideration. In choosing between finite horizons of varying lengths the considerations outlined earlier, together with the inevitable cumulation of uncertainties of a receding future, dictate the choice of a horizon which does not put off decisions for too long.

3. *Rate of Growth of Consumption within the Planning Period*
The rate at which consumption is allowed to grow during the plan is another element in the decision as to how to spread the benefits of economic development over time. Moreover, it affects in a direct way the rate of growth of production and of capital accumulation for further growth. The more quickly consumption is allowed to grow, and the lower the rate of saving out of the increments of production, then the greater the current spread of the benefits of development. Development itself, however, depends on the plowback of increased output into investment. So a too large or premature diversion to

production of consumption goods of the resources which become increasingly available as the result of development could stifle that development.

The decision as to what growth in consumption will be permitted is again a political one. Ordinarily in free societies it will be difficult to rule out at least some increase in consumption. As incomes rise and as unemployment, open and disguised, is reduced, there will be increasing demands for consumption goods.

Another major source of pressure will be the general upgrading of the working force which takes place as part of the process of development: increasing numbers of unskilled workers acquire skills; more persons move into foreman and supervisory status, become higher civil servants, managers, entrepreneurs, and so on. As individuals participate in this process of upgrading their occupations they will also try to upgrade their consumption to the patterns of the new levels they are achieving. Thus the mere maintenance of the present relative supplies of consumption goods will mean growing scarcities of particular types as increasing numbers of persons bid for the apartments, motor scooters, automobiles, etc. of the higher income levels. Denial of these amenities is in turn certain to become a pressing political issue.

The political and economic interconnections between the choice elements in long-term planning are illustrated by the relations between the choice of initial consumption levels and of the rate of growth of consumption during the plan. Suppose the initial level of aggregate consumption from which planning starts could be diminished by reduction of the inequalities of consumption. Subsequent upgrading of consumption as occupational levels rise would then mean less over-all pressure on consumption. On the other hand, the decision might be that current reduction of the inequalities of consumption is politically more difficult than delaying the upgrading process. Or there may be some planned use of both procedures.

From the standpoint of production possibilities there is great flexibility in the rates of consumption growth at various phases of a plan over the planning horizon: fast at first, slow later, or *vice versa* or any other pattern. Each pattern of growth rates and each composition would have a different economic significance and each would pose a different political problem. High consumption growth rates in the early plan stages may be justified not only on humane grounds but also on those of increasing human stamina or giving necessary encouragement for future sacrifices. On a political evaluation that it is more difficult to hold down consumption once it has begun to grow, just the reverse procedure might be dictated. The detail of alternative patterns of consumption growth must also be considered in order to have a full appreciation of their political as well as economic significance.

4. *Terminal Conditions in Planning*

Stipulation of the terminal conditions of an intertemporal plan requires the choice of one or another set of national economic goals. These terminal conditions may have alternative characterizations. For example, it may be specified as a political decision that at the end of the planning horizon certain minimum consumption levels should be achieved and that some particular rate of growth should be maintainable thereafter. Or it may be stipulated that a particular level of employment should be a terminal condition or that independence from external assistance be established by the end of the plan.

Of course it may not be possible for the economy to achieve whatever set of targets is specified. Or it may be possible to achieve the targets only by means of sacrifices in the other choice elements. There will be inter-relations also among the various components of the terminal conditions and possibilities of doing better in one sector by accepting a lower level of performance in another sector. There are detailed problems of economic analysis in determining the feasibility of the terminal conditions and their relations with each other as well as with other choice elements.

The particular year-by-year production targets of a plan are not terminal conditions in themselves. They are the implications of such conditions taken together with the values given to the other choice elements. The annual production levels emerge as the result of the total planning process.

The content of the terminal conditions is a political decision: the economic goals which it is the nation's objective to achieve by the end of the planning horizon. If the goals are specified in terms of consumption levels, then the politics of consumption levels and distribution are involved in an obvious way. Statements of terminal conditions in terms of resources of productive capacity, i.e. in terms of steel capacity or dams or power stations or machine tool production, have implications for consumption and saving as well and therefore are just as political. If the implications are hidden, the content of the political decisions may be obscure. It is possible that the statement of terminal conditions in terms of productive capacity raises fewer internal political issues just because the consumption, saving, and tax implications are unspecified, though not by any means undetermined.

The choice of terminal conditions for a planning period does not mean that there is a lack of concern for succeeding years. Rather it is a decision about the desired characteristics of an intermediate station in economic growth. These characteristics may include rewards for previous effort and provide also for more future growth depending on political evaluations and satisfaction of economic feasibility requirements.

In the replanning mentioned above the terminal conditions as well as the other choice elements of the intertemporal plan may be modified in the light of new alternatives which become available or new exigencies which must be faced. If a plan is made with standards of equity in mind and if it is regarded as a national compact, the new set of choices should, to the maximum extent possible, provide for no worse standards of life for the population and exploit to the fullest any new opportunities which arise.

II. SUBSTITUTION AMONG CHOICE ELEMENTS

The economic and technical limitations on the choice elements have already been referred to as they are inescapable characteristics. For example, the higher the value given to consumption in the initial conditions, the less the initial investment and the subsequent growth possibilities. The higher the intermediate rate of growth of consumption, all other things being equal, the less the achievement possible in the terminal conditions. The longer the planning horizon, the lower the initial investment necessary to reach any specified terminal conditions. The more ambitious the terminal conditions, the greater the need for stringency in consumption initially and/or through the planning period. These are straightforward qualitative conditions which arise out of the basic facts of limited resources and which do not require any specific planning framework for their revelation. In practical planning, of course, it is the exact quantitative nature of the limitations and substitution possibilities which are of great interest. To know these quantitative possibilities in detail requires a great deal of technical and economic information, the specification of a planning model, and a lot of computation. The basic logic can be illustrated simply, however, with an aggregate model whose objective is the achievement of consistency among the choice elements.

Suppose we think in terms of the production of a generalized output which is divided between consumption and investment. We start with the amount of resources available at the beginning of the plan. This availability in this aggregative approach is represented by the stock of capital and its productivity coefficient. As the first decision about one of the choice elements we might stipulate the initial levels of consumption and thus also determine the initial use of the available resources in the production of consumption goods and in capital formation. However, we provisionally leave this element to be determined by decisions about the other three choice elements. The terminal conditions will be translated into a specific level of capital stock to be reached at a particular time in the future. The choice of that time determines the planning horizon. Finally a decision must be made about the choice of the rate of growth of consumption which will be allowed during the plan period.

Not every possible path and set of parameters are consistent, which reflects the constraints of the economic system, but we shall consider only those which can be realized. The over-all productivity of capital will be taken to be close to that implicit in the Indian Third Five Year Plan. We also take the 1960-61 levels of consumption in India of roughly 14,000 crores of rupees as the basis for comparison with the initial levels of consumption derived from the planning model.

The significance of alternative decisions on the choice elements in long-term planning can now be illustrated by a set of numerical examples. The *planning horizon* is set at fifteen years. The *terminal condition* is at first set so that there is *no growth* in capital stock by the end of the planning period. Each row of Table I shows the necessary change in the *initial consumption* level as compared to that now prevailing as the result of a specification on the *rate of growth of consumption* allowed during the plan.[1] Thus, remembering that the rate of population growth in India is itself about 2 per cent, a small increase in consumption would be permissible immediately if it were intended that per capita consumption were to remain constant over the next fifteen years and if there were to be no change in the stock of productive resources by the end of the period. If the rate of growth of consumption is set at 4 per cent during the plan period, and everything else remains the same, then, in order to give a 2 per cent increase in per capita consumption, current consumption levels must be cut by 4·8 per cent. A 6 per cent rate of increase in consumption implies even greater current sacrifices.

Table I

Rate of Growth of Consumption during Plan Period	Required Change in the Initial Level of Consumption
2%	+ 0·4%
4%	− 4·8%
6%	−10·0%

A more ambitious terminal goal has more austere implications. If the objective is to *double the stock of capital goods* by the end of the 15 year plan period, i.e. to achieve an annual average rate of growth in capital resources of slightly less than 5 per cent, we have the conditions of Table II. That table indicates that the terminal goal is achievable with no sacrifice in the current or future levels of per capita consumption. But let the current level of consumption rise by ever so little, and that goal will not be achieved. If it rises by as much as 0·4 per cent, Table I says that the capital resources will just be maintained over the plan period. If per capita consumption is allowed to rise during the plan, then there must be greater *immediate* sacrifice if the terminal condition is to be achieved. There must be a sacrifice of 5 per cent in current consumption for a 4 per

[1] These tables are based on a simple aggregative model which is outlined in a brief Appendix.

cent intermediate rate of growth of consumption and an immediate sacrifice of 10 per cent for a 6 per cent rate of growth in consumption over the plan period.

Table II

Rate of Growth of Consumption during Plan Period	Required Change in the Initial Level of Consumption
2%	0·0%
4%	− 5·0%
6%	−10·2%

These examples are not intended to be descriptive, though they are approximative with respect to the Indian economy. They are illustrative of the significance of alternative inter-temporal planning decisions. They clearly demonstrate that what is done right now does make a great deal of difference for the future. Having a long-term plan, for example, does not encourage complacency or procrastination. Rather its purpose is to indicate what must be done immediately. In the present circumstances it suggests the need for great stringency in containing the pressures for raising consumption levels if the national goals are to be reached. This in turn implies the need for reviewing policies designed to restrict consumption at the upper-income levels in order to share the burdens of sacrifice equitably.

Changing the decision about the planning horizon is not in itself so important in determining the current and future levels of consumption permissible, as is shown in Table III for a planning horizon of twenty years. Of course this does not imply that the choice of a planning horizon may not be important on political and equity grounds as discussed above.

Table III

Rate of Growth of Consumption during the Plan Period	Required Change in the Initial Level of Consumption	
	If Capital Stock is not to Grow	If Capital Stock is to Double over the Plan Period
2%	+ 0·3%	+ 0·2%
4%	− 5·0%	− 5·0%
6%	−10·3%	−10·3%

III. OPTIMIZING PLANNING MODELS

The description of choice elements in intertemporal planning, as well as of the rates at which they can be substituted, has so far been based on a consistency planning model. This type of planning framework has as its major objective the maintenance of intertemporal and intersectoral consistency as the plan moves from its beginning to its end over the planning period, satisfying specified intermediate requirements. The choice element concept changes in the context of an optimizing model, however. To broaden the discussion it will be useful to turn briefly to such models whose goal is the immediate deduction of the best plan of development. It will be most convenient for the purposes of illustration to continue to deal with economic aggregates.

Two broad types of optimization models can be distinguished: (1) optimization models defined with respect to a terminal state, and (2) models in which the optimization procedure attempts to single out the best among all alternative paths. In the first type of model the objective is to find a plan which leads to the highest possible value of a function made up of the economic magnitudes which describe the terminal conditions. Examples of this are models which maximize terminal consumption or the utility of terminal consumption or some mix of terminal consumption and investment. These belong to what have become known as 'turnpike' type models. Compared to them the second type of optimization model takes into account the entire path leading from a specified initial position to a specified terminal position. Among the class of feasible paths it picks the one which is the best in terms of a stated preference function. These may be called Ramsay-type models after their original analyst.

In a turnpike-type optimization model the choice elements are the length of the planning horizon, the initial level of consumption, and the exact nature of the preference function involving the terminal variables. The intermediate rate of growth of consumption cannot be chosen also but must be deduced or there would be no scope left for the optimizing procedure. In a Ramsay-type planning model the choice elements are more intricate than in any of the alternative models discussed so far.

79

As in the consistency model, the planning horizon and terminal objectives are specified. The initial and intermediate levels of consumption emerge as part of the solution of the model. The other choice elements are in the definition of the preference function which must evaluate the utility of one entire consumption path against that of another. Composing a preference function with meaningful choice elements for this type of model is a difficult task.

IV. INTERTEMPORAL MULTI-SECTOR PLANNING

The basic components of intertemporal planning have been illustrated in terms of aggregate planning models. The next step is to elaborate these approaches in order to operate in the many-sector detail which constitutes the practical context of development programmes.

Expanding the scope of planning to many sectors also requires more detailed specification of each of the various choice elements. The initial conditions must now be described in terms of each of the items which make up the consumers' budget. The choice of a rate of growth of consumption now involves decisions about the different growth rates permitted for each one of these items at various stages over the plan period. The terminal conditions must also be specified in detail. Instead of stipulating only one level of aggregate consumption and aggregate investment in the terminal period, each of the consumption, investment, and other final output items must be indicated for that period. Only the planning horizon can continue to be given as a single number.

Detailed information is also required about the structural relations between the various sectors with respect both to their current requirements and to their requirements for capital expansion. Inter-industry or input-output information is an essential ingredient.

A multi-sector intertemporal planning model can be envisaged which is essentially an extension to many sectors of the simple aggregate consistency model already described. The result of the planning process would be the determination period-by-period of production levels or targets which are consistent with the decisions made about the choice elements.

80

The possibility of replanning would always be kept open. In fact the approach is envisaged as a continuing process which permits adjustments to take into account the actual levels of achievement year by year and changes in structural relations.

This type of planning procedure does what an intertemporal plan should do and tells what must be done now in order to achieve distant goals. The approach illustrated here is not one of general optimization, however, and would not attempt the ambitious task of finding the best of all possible paths of development. It would be desirable to explore the implications of alternative paths and in that way provide a basis for discrimination among them. Analyses of this type could also lead to the eventual use of optimization models to investigate the substitution possibilities among terminal conditions, for example, and, in this way, fuller exploration of the potentialities of economic development.

By no means all of the problems of intertemporal planning can be handled in any planning model. Much data collection and statistical estimation must be done outside it and fed into it. Results of the planning process must be interpreted and disaggregated. Fiscal and monetary issues have to be handled separately. Yet an intertemporal planning procedure provides the focus necessary to make all these separate activities coherent.

APPENDIX

The simple aggregative model underlying the numerical examples is familiar to economists. The following variables and parameters are used:

$Y(t)$ — National income or output in period t

$C(t)$ — total consumption in period t is $\bar{C}e^{rt}$ where $\bar{C}$ is the initial level of consumption and r the rate of growth of consumption chosen for the inter-plan period

$K(t)$ — the capital stock existing in period t

$I(t)$ — investment, or the change in capital stock, in period t or $K(t)$

b — the output-capital ratio, or $Y(t)/K(t)$, which is set at $1/2.5$ or 0.4

T — the planning period.

F

6

CAPITAL FORMATION:
A THEORETICAL AND
EMPIRICAL ANALYSIS[1]

R. S. ECKAUS
LOUIS LEFEBER

Many of the issues of economic growth and development must be analysed within the framework of capital theory. In this chapter we develop a model for inter-temporal choice in production which, though relatively simple, nonetheless contains some of the most important elements commonly encountered in economic planning and in the analysis of capital accumulation. Also, in order to demonstrate its empirical relevance we employ our theoretical results for the empirical estimation of the marginal rate of return over cost and other quantitative features of the United States economy.

We work at a high level of aggregation, distinguishing only between consumption and capital goods on the output side and between labour and capital on the input side. However, both the theory and the estimation procedures, as discussed below, would allow further disaggregation in the anslysis. Nevertheless, without trying to minimize the usefulness of more disaggregated models, we have purposely decided to present a two-sector approach. We have done so for several reasons. First, its concepts approximate the framework most frequently employed to analyse problems of economic growth. Secondly, at this stage the gaps in the data are such that multi-

[1] This is the outcome of both joint and independent research by the authors. They are indebted to Messrs A. Ando, S. Chakravarty, P. Rosenstein-Rodan, P. A. Samuelson and R. M. Solow for useful comments. Particular credit should be given to Mr Robert Coen for his excellent statistical work. However, the responsibility for errors belongs entirely to the authors. The authors gratefully acknowledge the support provided by the M.I.T. Center for International Studies as well as the financial aid given by the Rockefeller Foundation to R. S. Eckaus and by the Department of Economics, Harvard University, to L. Lefeber. (Originally without Appendix, published in *Review of Economics and Statistics*, May 1962.)

83

sector comparisons may not be warranted. Finally, our approach facilitates the analytical exposition which otherwise might not lend itself to simplified presentation.

The theoretical framework and analysis are described in Section I. Section II discusses the relationship between our approach and other models in capital theory developed in the past. The empirical application of the framework is presented in Section III.

I. THE ANALYTICAL FRAMEWORK

The framework consists of a simple non-linear programme based on the customary assumptions of convexity and continuity in the constraints. We consider the production of a consumption good $X^1(t)$ and of a homogeneous capital good $X^2(t)$ in each of two discrete time periods, given stocks of labour $L(t)$ in each period and given an initial stock of capital $\overline{KS^{(0)}}$. Both labour and capital are used in both lines of production. The capital available in period t is restricted to the existing capital stock at the end of the previous period $t-1$. Capital is non-substitutable for the consumption good; that is, $X^2(t)$ is a distinctly different product from $X^1(t)$ and is not consumable in the conventional sense of the term. The consumption good produced in any one period is fully consumed in the same period: inventories of $X^1(t)$ are assumed to be zero.[1]

Capital, however, depreciates in use. Depreciation in this context means that part of the capital employed in any one activity is consumed in some given proportion to the capital input itself. If $K^1(t)$ and $K^2(t)$ denote capital employed in the production of the two goods in any one period, $\beta^1(t)K^1(t)$ and $\beta^2(t)K^2(t)$ are the amounts depreciated in that period. We stipulate that $0 \leq \beta^1(t) < 1$; that is, depreciation in any one line of production cannot exceed the capital employed in that line of activity.[2] In order to derive a transformation surface

---

[1] This is strictly an assumption to simplify the exposition. Inventories can be readily built into the framework. The motivation for carrying inventories is twofold: (*a*) to overcome various frictions in the flow of goods, (*b*) to satisfy future demand at higher prices than those of today. We abstract from both of these possibilities.

[2] A fully general treatment of capital consumption should take into account time depreciation and the effect of variations in the proportions of factors. To avoid cluttering up our equations we have abstracted from both of these con-

corresponding to any stipulated level of terminal capital stock, $\overline{KS(2)}$, we maximize the objective function,

$$W_1X^1(1)+W_2X^1(2) \tag{1}$$

subject to the following conditions:

$$X^i(t)=F^i[L^i(t),\ K^i(t)] \qquad\qquad ; i=1,2;\ t=1,2; \tag{2}$$

$$\sum_i L^i(t)\leqq L(t) \qquad\qquad ; i=1,2;\ t=1,2; \tag{3}$$

$$\sum_i K^i(t)\leqq KS(t-1) \qquad\qquad ; i=1,2;\ t=1,2; \tag{4}$$

$$D(t)=\sum_i \beta^i(t)\ K^i(t) \qquad\qquad ; i=1,2;\ t=1,2; \tag{5}$$

$$KS(o)=\overline{KS(o)} \tag{6}$$

$$KS(1)-KS(o)-X^2(1)+D(1)\leqq 0; \tag{7}$$

$$KS(2)=\overline{KS(2)}; \tag{8}$$

$$KS(2)-KS(o)-X^2(1)-X^2(2)+D(1)+D(2)\leqq o. \tag{9}$$

All variables are stipulated to be greater than or equal to zero.[1] The constraints under (2) are the production functions of the two goods in the two periods. Constraints (3) show the distribution of labour and (4) the distribution of capital in each period. The constraints under (5) describe the total depreciation

---

siderations. However, for purposes of estimation, time depreciation is implied by the retention of the time designation on the β's. As far as the effects of varying proportions are concerned, the following relationships provide the general case. Denoting depreciation in the production of the ith good in each period by $D^i(t)$ we have $D^i(t)=\beta^i(t)X^i(t)$. However, the rate of depreciation, $\beta^i(t)$, must itself be a function of factor proportions denoted by the function

$$\beta^i(t)=\beta^i(t)\left[\frac{K^i(t)}{L^i(t)}\right]$$

Hence

$$D^i(t)=\beta^i(t)\left[\frac{K^i(t)}{L^i(t)}\right]X^i(t).$$

Of course, if the over-all first order homogeneity requirement in the constraints is to be preserved, the $\beta^i(t)$ function must be homogeneous of order zero.

[1] There is one added set of constraints which we do not introduce explicitly but mention now for future reference. This set represents the Hawkins-Simon conditions for our model which ensure the viability of the growth system. The conditions can be formalized by writing

$$F_k{}^2(t)-\beta^2(t)>0; t=1,2;$$

i.e. the net marginal productivity of capital in producing capital must be greater than zero.

of capital in each period. Constraint (6) indicates the available initial stock of capital. Constraint (7) shows the capital stock at the end of the first period after the initial capital stock is changed by the amount of net investment of that period. Constraint (8) indicates the stipulated terminal capital stock and constraint (9) shows the capital stock at the end of the second period after the initial endowment is changed by production and depreciation in the two periods.

For any given terminal capital stock $\overline{KS(2)}$ the variation of the arbitrarily chosen W's of the objective function will trace out a feasibility surface for consumption in the two periods. By assuming alternative values for KS(2) itself, we trace out a surface, not only for consumption, but also for capital formation.[1] This surface completely describes *all* alternative consumption and investment choices open to society in the two periods under consideration *irrespective of any subsequent finite or infinite number of periods which may follow after our terminal date.*

Since this surface is of central importance, we shall present a geometrical as well as an analytical interpretation. Figure 1 shows the inter-relationships between $X^1(1)$, $X^1(2)$ and the net addition to the total capital stock over both periods, $KS(2) - KS(0)$. For each stipulated terminal stock the consumption alternatives must be on an arc formed by the intersection of the three-dimensional feasibility surface with a plane that is parallel to the $X^1(1)$ and $X^1(2)$ axes and cuts the $[KS(2) - KS(0)]$ axis at the specified level. These arcs are transformation functions between today's and tomorrow's consumption.

To trace out the feasibility surface we first note that there must be an upper limit to the amount by which the capital stock can be increased over the original endowment. The limit is reached when all resources in both periods are devoted to the production of capital goods; hence, the production of consumer goods must, throughout, be zero. This is the case at the vertex marked F in Figure 1.

Stipulation of a somewhat smaller terminal capital stock than the one represented by F makes some resources available for the production of consumer goods in either the first or

---

[1] Alternatively we could include in the objective function the terminal capital stock as an arbitrarily weighted variable. The resulting surface would be identical.

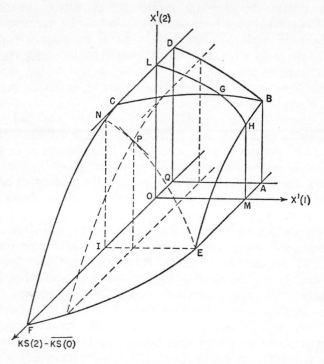

FIGURE 1

second periods. Such is the case, for example, at $KS(2)-KS(0)$ $=OI$. There might be IE of $X^1(1)$ produced and nothing of $X^1(2)$ or IN of $X^1(2)$ and nothing of $X^1(1)$, or a range of combinations between these extremes represented by the arc NE. Notice that IE equals OM, the maximum amount of consumer goods which can be produced in the first period when no resources are allocated to producing capital. Figure 1 shows that for the desired terminal stock implied by I and $X^1(1)=IE$ to be obtained, all resources must be allocated to produce capital goods in the second period; hence, production of $X^1(2)$ must be zero. If we chose to produce $X^1(1) <$ IE in the first period, some resources can be used to produce capital in that period and, correspondingly, some resources will be available to produce $X^1(2)$ in addition to the amounts needed to complete the stipulated terminal stock in the second period.

87

To obtain the terminal capital stocks within the range $I < KS(2)-KS(0) < F$ we cannot concentrate all our resources in the production of consumption goods in the first period. In this range the required total addition to capital stock exceeds the maximum net investment feasible in the second period. Hence, some capital must be produced already in the first period. This is shown by the arc EF.

In the range $Q \leqq KS(2)-KS(0) < I$ the required total addition to capital stock is sufficiently small that there is more leeway in the use of resources. Even if all factors were concentrated in the production of consumer goods in the first period, the stipulated additions to capital could be obtained in the second period and some consumer goods production as well. This is described by the arc EH.

Suppose the required total net addition to capital stock is zero and the maximum amount of X^1 (1), OM, is produced. Then in the second period we can produce both $X^1(2)=HM$ *and* enough capital to offset the depreciation incurred in both periods. If we reduce the production of $X^1(1)$ by moving from M toward O, we can increase the output of $X^1(2)$ along the arc GH, using the factors released in the first period for capital formation. At a given point, however, further investment to increase $X^1(2)$ results in so much capital accumulation that even after depreciation the terminal capital must exceed the initial stock. This point is reached at G. Past this point, on the arc GH, the terminal capital stock becomes a free good.

The terminal stock requirement can, of course, be smaller than the initial one. This is the case in the range $Q < KS(2)-KS(0) < 0$. If only consumer goods are produced in both periods, as represented by point B, the decrement OQ in capital stock must exactly equal the total depreciation.

In the triangular section BCD the terminal capital stock is redundant. The explanation is in the fact that capital goods production in the first period results in a higher 'left over' terminal capital stock than the one implied by any point selected on the surface of this region. Here the intersection of the surface with planes parallel to the $X^1(2)$ and $[KS(2)-KS(0)]$ axes defines straight lines of zero slope; that is, the price of the terminal stock relative to $X^1(2)$ is zero.[1]

---

[1] We abstract from disposal problems.

By similar reasoning we can show that in the region ABE both $X^1(2)$ and the terminal stock must have a zero price in terms of $X^1(1)$. Both of these regions, ABE and BCD, are particular manifestations of the 'fixed' nature of capital, that is, that capital does not fully depreciate in employment. For our analysis the relevant region is delineated by BCFE which is both convex and has continuous slopes in both directions. Within this region the consumption good and the terminal stock must have finite positive prices in both periods.

The selection of any one KS(2) is the expression of a long-term saving goal for society. But the stipulation of a terminal capital stock, barring the extreme case at F, leaves society with a second choice to make: how to allocate effort in the short run between investment and consumption goods in a manner consistent with that goal. For example, if the stipulated addition to capital stock is at I in the above Figure, that goal can be reached by a two-dimensional infinity of choices lying along the arc NE. The slope of that arc at any given point indicates the rate whereby tomorrow's consumption can be increased by foregoing some consumption today and by utilizing the factors thus released in the production of capital goods. By denoting this marginal rate of transformation of today's into tomorrow's consumption by $(1+r)$, we can identify r as Irving Fisher's well-known concept of 'marginal rate of return over cost' which in equilibrium must equal the market rate of interest. In our framework equilibrium is established if $(1+r)$ is brought into equality with the ratio of the arbitrary weights W_1/W_2, which in turn identically equals $(1+i)$, where i is the market rate of interest.

Underlying the maximization is a set of eight differential inequalities, one corresponding to each of the input variables. Denoting the partial change in $X^1(t)$ and $X^2(t)$ with respect to the two factors of production by $F^1_L(t)$, $F^1_K(t)$, $F^2_L(t)$ and $F^2_K(t)$, we have

$$W_1 F^1_L(1) \leq \lambda_L(1) \qquad ; \qquad (10)$$

$$[\lambda_K(2) + \lambda^k] F^2_L(1) \leq \lambda_L(1) \qquad ; \qquad (11)$$

$$W_2 F^1_L(2) \leq \lambda_L(2) \qquad ; \qquad (12)$$

$$\lambda^k F^2_L(2) \leq \lambda_L(2) \qquad ; \qquad (13)$$

$$W_1 F^1_K(1) - [\lambda_K(2) + \lambda^k] \beta^1(1) \leq \lambda_K(1) \qquad ; \qquad (14)$$

$$[\lambda_K(2) + \lambda^k][F^2_K(1) - \beta^2(1)] \leq \lambda_K(1) \qquad ; \qquad (15)$$

89

$$W_2 F^1_K(2) - \lambda^k \beta^1(2) \leq \lambda_K(2) \qquad ; \qquad (16)$$
$$\lambda^k [F^2_K(2) - \beta^2(2)] \leq \lambda_K(2) \qquad ; \qquad (17)$$

The set of the first four relationships (10) to (13) refers to the allocation of labour; the remaining ones (14) to (17) refer to the allocation of capital in the two periods. λ^k is the shadow price of the terminal stock, $\lambda_L(i)$ and $\lambda_K(i)$ are the net shadow prices of the two factors in the ith period.

It is interesting to observe the rent relationships contained by the differential inequations. The value of the marginal product of any factor is, of course, the product of the marginal physical product and of a price term. In this sense relationships (10), (12), and (13) are straightforward. However, notice, for example, in (11) that the price term itself is a sum of two prices, that is, that of the rent of capital in the second period and of the shadow price of the terminal stock. This is so because the capital produced in the first period will be available for use in the second period and will also contribute to the desired terminal capital stock.

In the constraints governing the allocation of capital, it should be noted that the Langrangean multipliers on the right-hand sides of the inequalities represent rents *net* of depreciation. The value of the marginal depreciation must be subtracted from the gross value of the marginal product of capital in order to obtain the *net* rent. Depreciation resulting in the first period is valued by a composite price term, since the 'lost' capital will not be available in the second period for producing either good, nor will it become a component part of the required terminal stock.

In the relationships (15) and (17), that is, in those which refer to the marginal productivity of capital in producing capital, the depreciation factor is subtracted directly from the marginal product in physical terms. This can be done because of our assumption that capital produced and depreciated is homogeneous. The difference of these two magnitudes, that is, of $F^2_K(t) - \beta^2(t)$, is the *net marginal physical* product of capital in producing capital.

We have stipulated earlier (see footnote 1, p. 85) that for the viability of the growth system, $F^2_K(t) - \beta^2(t) > 0$ must hold. This requirement is the Hawkins-Simon condition of the model.

The condition ensures that the marginal rate of transformation between alternative combinations of consumptions consistent with any one terminal capital stock, must exceed one for at least some portions of the feasibility surface. The rationale of the condition can be readily understood by a glance at the structure of the surface in Figure 1. Take for instance the transformation that corresponds to $KS(2)-KS(0)=OI$. Here, if the net marginal productivity of the factors producing capital is positive, then $IN>IE$; hence, the slope of a straight line between N and E must exceed one (in absolute value); hence, the arc NE must at least in the portion adjacent to E have a slope greater than one.

On the surface bounded by CFEB, that is, where both consumptions and the terminal stock have a positive finite value, all differential relationships must exactly satisfy the equality. Making use of all the relationships, we eliminate the multipliers and obtain the following equalities as conditions of a maximum:

$$\frac{W_1}{W_2}=\frac{F^1{}_L(2)}{F^1{}_L(1)}\frac{F^2{}_L(1)}{F^2{}_L(2)}\,[1+F^2{}_K(2)-\beta^2(2)];\qquad(18L)$$

$$\frac{W_1}{W_2}=\frac{F^1{}_K(2)}{F^1{}_K(1)}\frac{F^2{}_K(1)-\beta^2(1)+\beta^1(1)}{F^2{}_K(2)-\beta^2(2)+\beta^1(2)}[1+F^2{}_K(2)-\beta^2(2)]\qquad(18K)$$

Both equations have a common multiplicative term, that is, one plus the net marginal product of capital in producing capital. Otherwise equation (18L) is composed of marginal productivities of labour and equation (18K) of marginal productivities of capital. W_1/W_2 is, of course, identically equal to one plus the market rate of interest; hence, both ratios are expressions of the marginal transformation rate between consumptions.

Notice that if the marginal productivities and the depreciation rates were constant over time, after cancellation of terms in both numerator and denominator, the marginal rate of return over cost would equal the net marginal product of capital in producing capital.

Equations (18L) and (18K) are significant as they show the nature of the dependence of this transformation rate on the different marginal productivities and depreciation. For instance, the marginal rate of return over cost will be the greater the higher the marginal product of labour or capital in consumer goods production in the second period relative to that in the first period. On the other hand, the greater the marginal product of labour or capital in producing capital in the second period relative to that in the first period, the smaller will be the marginal rate of return over cost.

By combining equations (18L) and (18K) we obtain one of the familiar over-all efficiency conditions on the marginal productivities of capital and labour:[1]

[1] It should be noted that (19) is different from the general intertemporal conditions yielded by the Dorfman, Samuelson, Solow model with many produced goods and factors. See R. Dorfman, P. A. Samuelson, R. M. Solow, *Linear Programming and Economic Analysis* (New York, 1958), Chapter 12. In the model above, with the initial and terminal stocks of capital given, the total net output of capital is also determined. Then, if either consumption or capital goods production is specified in any one of the periods, everything else is also determined in both periods. Hence, all that is left is the maintenance of intratemporal efficiency. The condition obtained from the combination of (18L) and (18K) is essentially a result of the combination of two separately identifiable intratemporal conditions obtainable from elimination of the λ's in equations (10)–(17) such as:

$$\frac{F^1_L(2)}{F^1_K(2)} = \frac{F^2_L(2)}{F^2_K(2) - \beta^2(2) + \beta^1(2)} .$$

Introduction of another capital factor would create the need for satisfaction of essential intertemporal efficiency conditions. We would obtain an additional condition like (18K) with the new capital factor appearing in the final term which then would not cancel out.

It may improve the understanding of the condition if we derive it by way of common-sense reasoning based on the marginal adjustments which are needed to maintain an equilibrium position on the transformation surface. Holding the output of $X^1(1)$, the capital stock at the end of the first period and the variables of the second period, constant, one unit of capital, K, is shifted in the first period from producing capital to producing the consumption good. Thus

$$\Delta X^1(1) = F^1_L(1) \cdot \Delta L^1(1) + F^1_K(1) \cdot \Delta K^1(1) = 0.$$

Setting $\Delta K^1(1) = 1$, the offsetting change in the labour input becomes

$$\Delta L^1(1) = -\left(F^1_K(1) \Big/ F_L(1) \right)$$

Since

$$\Delta L^2(1) = -\Delta L^1(1) \text{ and } \Delta K^1(1) = -\Delta K^2(1) = 1,$$

the change in the production of capital can be written as

$$\Delta X^2(1) = F^2_L(1) \cdot \Delta L^2(1) + F^2_K(1) \cdot \Delta K^2(1)$$

$$= F^2_L(1)\left(F^1_K(1) \Big/ F^1_L(1) \right) - F^2_K(1).$$

$$\frac{F^1_L(2)}{F^1_L(1)} \quad \frac{F^2_L(1)}{F^2_L(2)} \quad \frac{F^1_K(2)}{F^1_K(1)} \quad \frac{F_K(1)-\beta^2(1)+\beta^1(1)}{F^2_K(2)-\beta^2(2)+\beta^1(2)} \tag{19}$$

In addition to conditions of the form in equations (18) we can find other interesting relationships among the different rents and prices. The rate at which current consumption is given up for terminal capital stock is one of them:

$$\frac{\lambda^k}{W_2} = \frac{F^1_L(2)}{F^2_L(2)} \quad ; \tag{20L}$$

$$\frac{\lambda^k}{W_2} = \frac{F^1_K(2)}{F^2_K(2)-\beta^2(2)+\beta^1(2)} \cdot \tag{20K}$$

These are ratios between the marginal products of the factors in producing consumer goods on the one hand and their contribution to the accumulation of the terminal capital stock on the other hand.[1] The latter, in the case of the application of labour, is equal to the marginal product of labour in producing capital; in the case of capital, however, depreciation in producing consumer goods must be also taken into account if the entire marginal change in the capital stock is to be registered.

Apart from indicating the relative weight put on having a given terminal stock *vis-à-vis* consumption, equations (20) would be significant if the terminal stock were treated as a variable rather than a parameter. Though λ^k would be replaced by an arbitrary weight, the expressions would remain the same,

---

The capital stock at the end of the first period must remain unaffected by marginal changes in the production and use of capital in the various lines; hence these changes must all balance out. Thus

$$\Delta KS(1)=\Delta X^2(1)+\beta^2(1)\Delta K^2(1)-\beta^1(1)\Delta K(1)=0.$$

Substituting for $\Delta X^2(1)$, $\Delta K^2(1)$ and $\Delta K^1(1)$, we have

$$F^2_L(1)\left(F^1_K(1)\Big/ F^1_L(1)\right)-F^2_K(1)+\beta^2(1)-\beta^1(1)=0.$$

This can be rearranged in the form:

$$\left(F^1_K(1)\Big/ F^1_L(1)\right) \cdot \left(F^2_L(1)\Big/ F^2_K(1)-\beta^2(1)+\beta^1(1)\right)=1.$$

By similar reasoning for the second period we can obtain the analogous condition

$$\left(F^1_K(2)\Big/ F^1_L(2)\right) \cdot \left(F^2_L(2)\Big/ F^2_K(2)-\beta^2(2)+\beta^1(2)\right)=1.$$

By equating the two left-hand sides of the conditions for each period and re-arranging terms we obtain the conditions expressed in (19).

[1] No corresponding rate needs to be written out for consumption in period 1 as expressions (18) and (20) jointly determine it.

93

and jointly with (18) would fix our exact position on the feasibility surface.[1]

In either case it is important to note that the stipulation of a rate of interest in itself is insufficient to yield a unique optimum solution as *there is an infinity of alternative terminal capital stocks consistent with any one given interest rate.* To obtain a solution, either the terminal capital stock itself or the price of capital in terminal stock relative to consumption must be given *in addition* to the rate of interest. Considered in this light *the role of the rate of interest is to guide allocation of effort between producing consumption goods and capital in each time period toward the fulfilment of an ultimate goal.* The latter can be determined exogenously, that is, independent of the rate of interest, or endogenously, in which case the rate of interest will be a partial determinant of the goal as well as a guide to its attainment.

II. ANALYTICAL BACKGROUND

In order to analyse the choices between consumption and the formation of fixed capital, we have derived an intertemporal feasibility surface and we have obtained all-important conditions for the optimal distribution of resources given final prices in each time period.

Our approach, of course, was determined by the objective of our investigations. In terms of *analytical purpose* our effort is most closely related to the work of Irving Fisher.[2] However, we do not deal with the demand side where Fisher's most important contribution lies. We confine ourselves to the deriva-

---

[1] In a somewhat more general formulation, assume the existence of a social welfare function which includes the terminal capital stock as well as consumptions:

$$W = W[X^1(1), X^1(2), KS(2)].$$

Then the ratios of the partials,

$$\frac{\dfrac{\partial W}{\partial X^1(1)}}{\dfrac{\partial W}{\partial X^1(2)}} \quad \text{and} \quad \frac{\dfrac{\partial W}{\partial KS(2)}}{\dfrac{\partial W}{\partial X^1(2)}}$$

brought into equality with the corresponding ratios on the supply side, that is, (18) and (20) respectively, yield the maximum solution along with a corresponding rate of interest and price ratio between consumption and the final capital stock.

[2] Irving Fisher, *The Theory of Interest* (New York, 1930).

tion of the alternatives open to society and the optimality conditions on the supply side and we represent demand only by relative weights. It is probably fair to say that had Fisher concerned himself with fixed rather than circulating capital he would have constructed for the analysis of production a framework not dissimilar to ours.

While our purpose most closely agrees with that of Fisher, our analytical framework is rooted in the approach that was recently developed, particularly by the contributions of Dorfman, Samuelson, and Solow.[1] In fact, the model presented here can be interpreted as a special case of the Dorfman-Samuelson-Solow analysis of capital theory.

In addition, it is interesting to note the similarities and differences between the structural details of our analysis and other capital models. As our analysis focuses on the alternatives open on the production side, we do not 'close' our model by determining consumption as some given fixed proportion of output or by providing some alternative arbitrary decision rule. By comparison, the analytically important Ramsey model, in which there is only one good used either for consumption or investment, is closed by a condition on consumption.[2] The Ramsey objective, however, was the determination of an optimum saving programme and not the derivation of the range of alternative production programmes made possible by investment in durable capital. Similarly the advanced, many-sector theory of Samuelson and Solow presented in the paper, 'A Complete Capital Model Involving Heterogeneous Capital Goods', is 'closed' on the consumption side.[3]

The many-sector model of von Neumann is also closed; hence it does not make possible the exploration of the full range of feasible patterns of output over time.[4] Von Neumann investigated the characteristics of a special type of balanced growth equilibrium given the condition that all goods must have the

[1] Dorfman, Samuelson and Solow, *op. cit.*, especially Chapters 11 and 12. Other references are given below.

[2] Frank Ramsey, 'A Mathematical Theory of Saving', *Economic Journal*. XXXVIII (December 1928), 543–559.

[3] P. A. Samuelson and R. M. Solow, 'A Complete Capital Model Involving Heterogeneous Capital Goods', *Quarterly Journal of Economics*, LXX (November 1956), 537-562.

[4] John von Neumann, 'A Model of General Equilibrium', *Review of Economic Studies*, XIII (1) (1945-6), 1-9.

dual character of being both produced inputs and outputs. Consumption goods in his model are, in fact, no more than inputs necessary to produce the labour factor. If this assumption is dropped we move toward the framework of the model presented above; but then some of the striking results of the von Neumann analysis disappear, specifically the uniqueness of the 'balanced' and 'optimal' growth rate.[1]

Our treatment of capital can certainly not claim to cover all of its aspects. We operate with a simplified concept of depreciation in which, unlike Wicksell or in Solow's capital model, durability is not explicitly a choice variable.[2] Depreciation occurs as an element in the von Neumann and some other capital models in a form which cannot easily be related to reality: depreciated capital is one of the joint products of processes into which the undepreciated capital is an input.[3] Of course, in some capital models depreciation is avoided completely by operating only with net productivities as the result of an implicit depreciation deduction from gross productivities or by dealing only with 'working' or 'circulating' capital concepts.

In addition to allowing no variation in durability with respect to inputs, given a certain output, the model contains only a simple lag structure. Inputs in the production of consumption goods have instantaneous outputs, but capital goods produced in one period become available for use only in the succeeding period. Variations in the lag structure by type of capital could, of course, be introduced.

[1] J. G. Kemeny, O. Morganstern, and G. L. Thompson, 'A Generalization of the von Neumann Model of an Expanding Economy', *Econometrica*, XXIV (April 1956).

[2] Knut Wicksell, *Lectures on Political Economy*, I (London, 1949); R. M. Solow, 'Notes Toward a Wicksellian Model of Distributive Shares', International Economic Association, *The Theory of Capital*, ed. by F. A. Lutz and D. C. Hague (New York, 1961). Another path-breaking paper of Solow, 'Technical Change and the Aggregate Production Function', *The Review of Economics and Statistics*, XXXIX (August 1957), introduces technical change explicitly into a single commodity dynamic model. In our case, such changes are not incorporated into the model and can be represented only by the modest assumption of allowing production functions as well as the depreciation coefficients to be different from period to period.

[3] Actually, in the relationships (9) to (16) we could give a 'joint product' interpretation to capital rents. However, this would add little to clarity or empirical applicability.

By confining the model to a single capital good we expose ourselves to criticism of the type advanced by Mrs Robinson.[1] We could take refuge in such devices as Trevor Swan's *meccano* sets[2] but we prefer not to do so and defend ourselves on other grounds.[3] It is a matter of analytical and empirical convenience to have one capital and one consumption good: otherwise we could not draw the diagram in Figure 2 or present the empirical results in the form as they appear in Section III. Many capital and consumption goods would reveal more about internal structure, *à La Leontief*, but we forgo that type of analysis.[4] The Dorfman, Samuelson, Solow model, referred to above, is admirably suited to the investigation of such matters.

However, there is no point in claiming more or less generality for our approach. It is intended to be a simple approximation to choice problems as they are often seen in projections of economic growth. That it has empirical relevance must be demonstrated. This we shall attempt in the next section.

III. EMPIRICAL APPLICATION

The purpose of this section is the measurement of the marginal rates of return over cost in the United States for the ten-year period beginning 1947. These can be obtained from estimates of the transformation rates (18L) and (18K) on successive inter-period feasibility surfaces which mount up like the layers of an onion.

The results of our estimation are shown in the accompanying charts and table. The latter contains all the information, that is, the marginal productivities of factors and depreciation rates as well as the transformation rates themselves.

---

[1] J. Robinson, *The Accumulation of Capital* (London, 1956).

[2] T. Swan, 'Economic Growth and Capital Accumulation', *Economic Record* XXXII (November 1956).

[3] See P. A. Samuelson and R. Solow, 'A Complete Capital Model Involving Heterogeneous Capital Goods', *Quarterly Journal of Economics*, LXX (November 1956), 537-562.

[4] The model of Section I is also related analytically to the Marx and Ricardo-like systems developed by Professor Samuelson in 'Wages and Interest: Marxian Economic Models', *American Economic Review*, XLVII (December 1957), 884-912, and 'A Modern Treatment of the Ricardian Economy', *Quarterly Journal of Economics*, LXXIII (February and May 1959), 1-35 and 217-231 respectively.

Table 1

SUMMARY OF ESTIMATES

	1947	1948	1949	1950	1951	1952	1953	1954	1955	1956	1957
(1) $F_L^1(t)$	2·850	2·826	2·869	3·037	3·064	3·206	3·403	3·403	3·513	3·581	3·597
(2) $F_L^2(t)$	3·509	3·473	3·462	3·641	3·723	3·806	3·979	3·964	4·104	4·169	4·170
(3) $F_K^1(t)$	0·1396	0·1485	0·1407	0·1542	0·1577	0·1521	0·1493	0·1435	0·1532	0·1493	0·1461
(4) $F_K^2(t)$	0·2275	0·2414	0·2288	0·2616	0·2732	0·2524	0·2530	0·2365	0·2679	0·2571	0·2447
(5) $\beta^1(t)$	0·0214	0·0219	0·0241	0·0240	0·0243	0·0257	0·0270	0·0285	0·0293	0·0295	0·0295
(6) $\beta^2(t)$	0·0392	0·0401	0·0454	0·0444	0·0444	0·0487	0·0527	0·0583	0·0620	0·0609	0·0588
(7) W_1/W_2 based on (18L)		1·2036	1·2052	1·2251	1·2125	1·2320	1·2186	1·1827	1·2024	1·2004	1·1910
(8) W_1/W_2 based on (18K)		1·2006	1·2062	1·1476	1·1976	1·2809	1·1891	1·2454	1·1314	1·2148	1·2160
(9) λ^k/W_2 based on (20L)	0·8122	0·8137	0·8287	0·8341	0·8230	0·8424	0·8552	0·8585	0·8560	0·8590	0·8626
(10) λ^k/W_2 based on (20K)	0·6657	0·6653	0·6781	0·6393	0·6231	0·6630	0·6568	0·6942	0·6514	0·6615	0·6783

A THEORETICAL AND EMPIRICAL ANALYSIS

Estimation based on the model involves aggregation to two factors and two goods in addition to the ascription of our abstract assumptions to the real world. If the world would be 'perfect' and if exact statistical information would exist, estimates of (18L) and (18K) would have to be identical to each other. In terms of ten-year averages the marginal rate of return over cost for the years covered amounts to ·2030 when computed by substitution in equation (18K) and ·2074 when computed on the labour side, that is, using equation (18L). However, a glance at Figure 1 is sufficient to see that the ideal identity is not approximated by our yearly estimates. Unfortunately, we would have to know much more than we currently do in order to evaluate the role of 'imperfections' relative to the shortcomings of estimation in causing the discrepancies. It is sufficient to say that our estimates are only crude approximations of reality and that they reflect the weaknesses of both data and procedures.[1]

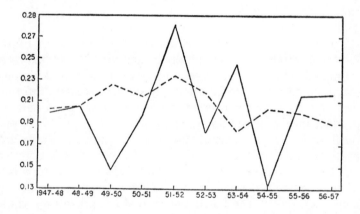

CHART 1

[1] The estimates presented here should be considered preliminary. Most of the more recent information such as contained in R. W. Goldsmith's important forthcoming work entitled *National Wealth of the United States in the Postwar Period*, to be published by the National Bureau of Economic Research Inc., was not available for our original computations. We are now engaged in revising our statistical methods and basic data. This we do in co-operation with Professor Albert Ando who has an interest in a similar statistical approach and who has already been helpful in improving our estimates.

99

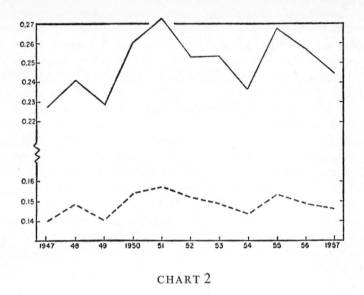

CHART 2

To obtain our results the marginal productivities of the factors in producing capital and consumption goods had to be estimated. There is, of course, no ready breakdown of national income data which would directly yield the necessary information. We have first converted the conventional gross national product into a private domestic concept and recorded the proportions going into consumption and investment.[1] These proportions were, in turn, applied year by year to the domestic private national income (in constant 1954 dollars) to obtain total incomes generated in producing investment goods and consumer goods. The income generated in agriculture, wholesale and retail trade, finance, insurance and real estate was credited entirely to consumption productions. The remainder of the national income earned in producing consumption was then allocated to the mining, manufacturing, transportation, construction, communication and public utility sectors. The residual of the national income created in these sectors was credited to capital production.

---

[1] Government purchases from the private sector are included as privately produced outputs.

100

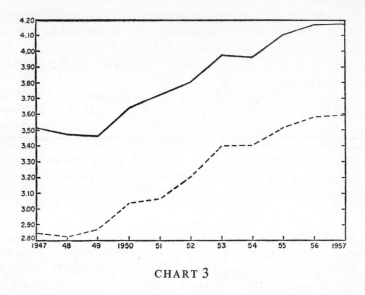

CHART 3

The allocation of the labour force and capital stock between consumption goods and capital production was done sector by sector in the same proportion as the division of income. Wages and gross rents (that is, profits, rents, interest and capital consumption allowances) were distributed between earnings in capital and consumption goods production by the same method.[1]

[1] The detailed steps of our estimation cannot be reproduced because of editorial limitations on space. However, in this note we shall try to indicate the procedure in order to underline the difficulties of developing the required data.

Wage bill information, sector by sector, was available from *US Income and Output*, US Department of Commerce (1958), with some necessary imputations of wages in the non-corporate sector. The total returns allowable to capital were estimated sector by sector as the residual after subtracting wages from the sum of national income and recorded depreciation. Total labour force figures were taken from Department of Commerce sources. Capital stock estimates had to be developed sector by sector, relying mainly on the Department of Commerce estimates, the National Bureau of Economic Research Studies in Capital Formation and Financing, and other sources. No capital estimates could be found, however, for the construction sector, and to obtain one, a fixed capital-output ratio was applied to the income generated in this sector.

In order to eliminate cyclical fluctuations in inventory stocks we have taken the average inventory-output ratios over the period covered and applied the latter annually to determine the inventory component of capital used by the different sectors.

The sectoral distribution of outputs and factor returns between capital and

101

Our marginal productivities were computed from the figures obtained by the above procedures.[1] The depreciation factors were calculated as the ratio of capital consumption allowances to income generated augmented by the same capital consumption allowances.

We have pointed out earlier that given perfect estimation and an economy which corresponds to our model, the two alternative estimates would have to give identical results. One of the important causes of the observed discrepancies lies in the cyclical behaviour of the economy. Our model is based on the implicit assumption of full employment, that is, that the economy operates on the intertemporal transformation surface. Although there was no 'great depression' during the period covered, there were several recessions.

It is to be expected that cyclical imperfection should show up more in the variability of the marginal productivity estimates of capital than that of labour.[2] As seen in Chart 1, this is reflected in the greater variability of the marginal rate of return estimates based on equation (18K) which are computed exclusively with the help of capital marginal productivities.

The cyclical changes in the marginal rates of return over cost estimates are not, however, related to the cycles in any simple way. Possibly because of the reasons cited in the previous footnote, the marginal productivities of capital, and with them estimates of (18K), vary directly with the business cycle. There are, however, conflicting cyclical influences in the marginal productivities of labour. Furthermore, they show a marked trend during the period covered. Both facts cause movements in the estimates based on (18L) that conflict with the pattern of the cycles.

---

consumer goods production as described above, neglects the contributions of agriculture and service industries to the production of capital and thus overstates the contribution of the other sectors in this respect. However, we feel that the above division introduces a less important error than the alternative possibility, i.e. the division of only aggregate rather than sectoral totals to consumption and capital goods production.

[1] Since we have assumed first order homogeneity in the production functions, the marginal products were estimated by the factors' average earnings.

[2] This is so partly because capital is a fixed factor and partly because profits are measured as a residual as opposed to wage rates which have an inflexibility downward.

102

Reference to the equations will recall that the marginal rate of return over cost is largely the result of ratios composed of present and future productivities. Changes in the marginal productivities of labour and capital have opposite effects depending on whether they occur in capital or consumer goods production. For a penetrating analysis of the cyclical behaviour of and the discrepancies between the estimates, however, the data underlying the estimation will have to be refined.[1]

Our estimates for the marginal rate of return are above the rates of return to capital commonly cited as effective in the American economy. Apart from the fact that our figures represent *marginal* rates rather than average profits, they also account for *all* returns to capital, that is, interests and rents as well as profits. Furthermore, they are measured before taxes (but after depreciation).[2] It would be more proper to compare our estimates with the yields on new investment, or to be exact, investment on the margin. If the latter were significantly below our estimates, the difference would represent the gap between socially realized and privately expected rates of return. This, in turn, would be a reflection of the difference between private and social risk and/or of the fact that the benefits of technological progress included in the observed rates may neither be fully foreseen nor fully realized by new investors.

APPENDIX

The estimation of the real rate of interest—i.e. the marginal rate of return over cost—was also undertaken for the Netherlands and for India. The computations were based on the same theoretical and analogous statistical methods as for the United States. The results are given below. As in the case of the computations for the United States, these are at best crude approximations.

The information necessary for the estimates is readily avail-

---

[1] We have also undertaken the estimation of the rates (20K) and (20L). The results are shown in Table 1. These show a more marked discrepancy than the figures discussed above. The estimates represent the rate of substitution between capital stock and consumption. They are, of course, not pure numbers and they do not readily lend themselves to empirical interpretation.

[2] The marginal rate of return implicit in Solow's model for technological change (*op. cit.*) is about 17 per cent. (Author's communication.)

103

able for the Netherlands.[1] Exactly as in the estimating procedure for the United States, the many sector information was aggregated into two sectors and labour and capital were allocated to the production of consumption and capital goods. The returns of the factors and the depreciation of capital were treated similarly. The marginal productivities of the factors were estimated by their average returns and substituted into the equations (18L) and (18K) as before.

Calculated by (18L) the marginal rate of return over cost averages 0·172 for the period 1948 through 1956; using (18K), composed only of the marginal productivities of capital, the average for the period is 0·135. If the extremely low estimate for 1952-3 were omitted, the average of the estimates based on (18K) would rise to 0·162. However, as seen in Chart 6, the estimates based on (18K) fluctuate more widely and, as in the case of the United States, do not always move in the same direction as the estimates based on (18L).

The estimates of the marginal productivities of labour have a fairly stable pattern; hence sharp movements in estimates of (18L) must be due primarily to fluctuations in the marginal product of capital in producing capital. These fluctuations would be, of course, exaggerated in our estimates because no adjustments were made to compensate for the cyclical under-utilization of capacity while labour unemployment is automatically accounted for by the data. At the same time there is a noticeable stability in the marginal productivity of capital in the consumer goods sector, which is undoubtedly due to anti-cyclical compensating fiscal policy. For instance, in the year 1952, there was a marked fall in net private fixed capital formation (strikingly reflected by our marginal productivity of capital estimates in the capital sector) in spite of which aggregate national income and with it the marginal product of capital in the consumer goods sector remained stable. After 1952 there was a sustained period of rapid capital formation—duly reflected in the estimates—which was accompanied by a milder increase in the marginal productivity of capital in the consumer goods sectors.

[1] The data was abstracted from the following sources prepared by the Netherlands Central Bureau of Statistics: *Nationale rekeningen*, 1958; *De produktestructuur van de Nederlandse volkshuishouding*, Deel 1. *'Input-Output' tabellen*, 1948–56; *Statistical Studies*, No. 9, 1959.

Table 2

SUMMARY OF ESTIMATES—NETHERLANDS

	1948	1949	1950	1951	1952	1953	1954	1955	1956
(1) $F_L^1(t)$	2·191	2·157	2·117	2·075	2·147	2·283	2·441	2·616	2·757
(2) $F_L^2(t)$	2·841	2·792	2·760	2·710	2·855	3·051	3·159	3·304	3·472
(3) $F_K^1(t)$	0·1006	0·1087	0·1107	0·1099	0·1116	0·1168	0·1234	·01312	0·1295
(4) $F_K^2(t)$	0·1597	0·1797	0·1816	0·1752	0·1590	0·2057	0·2037	0·2467	0·2591
(5) $\beta^1(t)$	0·0249	0·0255	0·0258	0·0260	0·0260	0·0261	0·0263	0·0269	0·0266
(6) $\beta^2(t)$	0·0335	0·0341	0·0345	0·0340	0·0315	0·0322	0·0332	0·0363	0·0363
(7) W_1/W_2 based on (18L)		1·1477	1·1389	1·1393	1·1074	1·1677	1·2087	1·2402	1·2263
(8) W_1/W_2 based on (18K)		1·0931	1·1561	1·1703	1·2487	0·0945	1·2542	1·0672	1·1484

Table 3

SUMMARY OF ESTIMATES—INDIA

					1950	1951	1952	1953	1954	1955	1956	1957
$F_K^1(t)$	:	:	:	:	0·2597	0·2308	0·2367	0·2288	0·2337	0·2303	0·2240	0·2234
$F_K^2(t)$	:	:	:	:	0·2596	0·2322	0·2360	0·2303	0·2357	0·2299	0·2250	0·2240
$\beta(t)$	:	:	:	:	0·0256	0·0255	0·0261	0·0257	0·0249	0·0250	0·0242	0·0236
W^1/W^2 based on (18K)	:					1·199	1·221	1·193	1·208	1·217	1·193	1·202

The estimates over the period 1952–53 to 1955–56 show divergent patterns. The shortness of the series does not permit judgments as to future behaviour, but it is notable that after 1954 the estimates appear to indicate convergence.

2. India[1]

The statistical information required to carry out the estimation is not directly available for the Indian economy. In addition to standard sources (Census of Manufacturers, Government White Papers on national income and statistical sample surveys) unpublished material had to be utilized to form the basis of the estimates. In certain areas, as for instance in estimating market activities not covered by sample surveys, cautious judgments were unavoidable.

The theoretical framework and basic statistical approach was the same as in the previous cases. Extension of the ordinary economic concept of labour employment is questionable in a

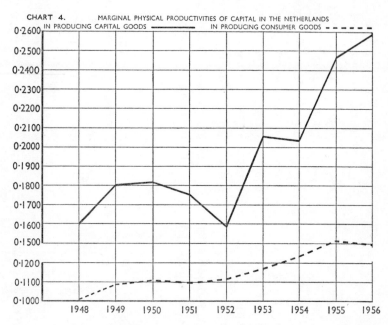

CHART 4. MARGINAL PHYSICAL PRODUCTIVITIES OF CAPITAL IN THE NETHERLANDS
IN PRODUCING CAPITAL GOODS ———— IN PRODUCING CONSUMER GOODS – – – – –

[1] The computation was done by Mr G. V. L. Narasimham of the Perspective Planning Division, Indian Planning Commission.

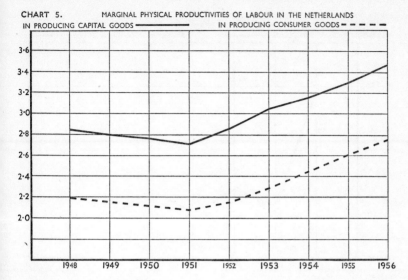

CHART 5.   MARGINAL PHYSICAL PRODUCTIVITIES OF LABOUR IN THE NETHERLANDS
IN PRODUCING CAPITAL GOODS ━━━━━   IN PRODUCING CONSUMER GOODS ━ ━ ━ ━

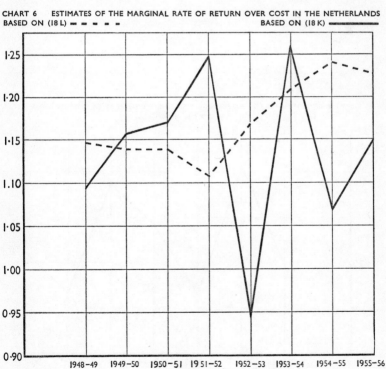

CHART 6   ESTIMATES OF THE MARGINAL RATE OF RETURN OVER COST IN THE NETHERLANDS
BASED ON (18 L) ━ ━ ━ ━ ━   BASED ON (18 K) ━━━━━

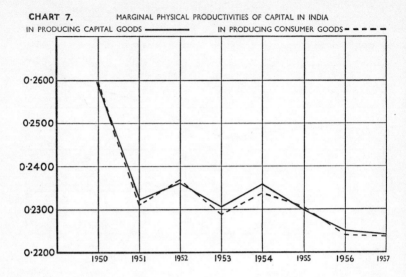

CHART 7.　　MARGINAL PHYSICAL PRODUCTIVITIES OF CAPITAL IN INDIA
IN PRODUCING CAPITAL GOODS ————————　　IN PRODUCING CONSUMER GOODS ▬ ▬ ▬ ▬

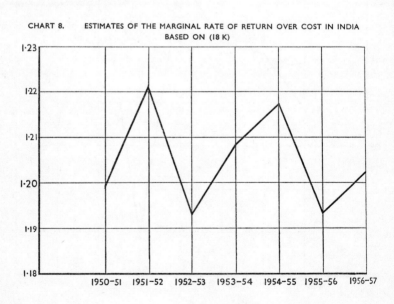

CHART 8.　　ESTIMATES OF THE MARGINAL RATE OF RETURN OVER COST IN INDIA
BASED ON (18 K)

significant part of Indian economic activity. Hence the estimation of the real rate of interest by (18L) was not undertaken. Furthermore, due to insufficient information the depreciation factors in the two sectors were assumed to be equal.

The estimates are summarized in Table 3 and the accompanying charts. The average rate of interest is 20·47 per cent for the period 1949 to 1957. The individual yearly estimates demonstrate considerable stability over time, as compared to the two other countries discussed above. The marginal productivities of capital underlying the estimates are themselves relatively stable and are fairly similar in size in the two sectors.

7

AN APPROACH TO A MULTI-SECTORAL INTERTEMPORAL PLANNING MODEL

S. CHAKRAVARTY

R. S. ECKAUS

I. CHOICE ELEMENTS IN MULTI-SECTORAL PLANNING

1. *The length of the planning horizon*

The choice elements in the multi-sectoral model are qualitatively the same as in the previously discussed case of an aggregative model, but they are now more numerous because of the necessity to interpret some of the variables in the present case as vector variables. We have the following list of choice elements:

(a) The length of the planning horizon, which may still be represented by a single number.

(b) The amounts and composition of the terminal capital stocks.

(c) The rate of growth of consumption during the planning period, which must also be interpreted as a vector because we have diverse consumer goods.

(d) The initial levels from which consumption of different items are allowed to rise.

Initial levels of capital stock in the different sectors of the economy are assumed as before as part of the data.

Interrelationships between choice elements constrain our movement in such a fashion that if we specify any three of the elements (a), (b), (c), and (d), the fourth is automatically determined. Once we know elements (a)–(d), the entire time path of output and capital accumulation (both in the vector sense) is determined over the planning period.[1]

The above description suggests that the keynote of this model is consistency and not optimization. Following the specification of three of the choice elements, the objective is to find, if it

---

[1] Since the time horizon is a single number while the other choice elements are vectors.

exists at all, the fourth set which makes them all consistent. In finding this solution the annual levels of output and sectoral allocations of output and investment are determined, and thus a plan is made in which all the parts are consistent with each other and the choice elements which have been fixed. Investigation of the consequences of alternative time paths of output may be carried out by use of this approach even without introducing optimization as an explicit part of the picture. This can be done by exploring the implications of alternative specifications of three of the four choice elements by means of successive solutions. Alternative rates of growth for the vector of consumption can be investigated or different assumptions can be made about the terminal position desired. For each specification we can derive the corresponding time pattern of output and accumulation. The policy-maker can then decide as to which particular configuration pleases him most.

All such solutions will be characterized by the full use of available capacity or a constant proportion of excess capacity. This raises the important question as to whether these are acceptable features of a planning model. Clearly a more general formulation involving varying degrees of excess capacity could have solutions which, with a proper specification of the preference function in an optimizing model, would dominate the solution corresponding to the no- or constant-excess-capacity case. In other words, we may have sets of substitution rates among various desired objectives for which the best procedure is to have some capital idle for some period. To handle such a general situation we would need to formulate our planning problems in an explicitly optimizing framework. Since the solution of a proper dynamic programming model is beyond our immediate purpose, the extra possibilities opened up by relaxing the equational structure of the model may be temporarily ignored. However, the test of consistency alone would require that the proper non-negativity conditions are obeyed by all the variables throughout the planning period.

The object of this paper is to demonstrate how a consistent solution can be found following specification of: (*a*) the length of the planning horizon, (*b*) the terminal output levels, and (*c*) the intermediate rates of growth of consumption. The discussion starts with a closed economy and with an unchanging set of structural coefficients. It then goes on to consider problems created by the variability of coefficients and, finally, indicates how the model may be adapted to deal with problems of international trade.

2. *Description of the initial state*

There are many alternative ways of describing an initial state for a particular economy. Naturally, the specific description chosen will correspond to the nature of the model which is going to be set up. Since our primary interest is in the pattern of production in the different sectors of the economy, one natural choice would have been to choose the levels of output in the different sectors in the initial year. But if we are interested in long-term planning, the proper state variables would be indicated not by the initial output levels but by the full capacity levels of output. Further, if we assume away excess capacity over the planning period, we can translate if we wish the full capacity levels of output into equivalent estimates of capital stock provided that capital-output ratios are known in advance. However, because of the simplifying assumptions made in this paper, it is a matter of relative indifference whether we use capital stock variables or output variables in describing the state of the economy.

3. *Description of the terminal state*

The terminal state is described in terms of a set of output levels desired for the terminal year. By the very nature of our model we have what mathematicians call a two-point boundary value problem, which implies that variables describing the initial and end configurations are qualitatively the same. In our case these variables constitute a vector $X(T)$, having the same dimensionality as $X(0)$. The final bill of goods in the terminal period, in addition to consumption, will provide for government purchase, capital formation, and exports. Now how do we determine this vector $X(T)$? To be sure, there is an unavoidable element of arbitrariness about this choice.

There are various possible types of end configurations that we may want to arrive at. Corresponding to any particular choice, we have the technical problem of translating this description into an equivalent description involving the $X(T)$'s.

Thus, if the consumption vector is to be set as a target, we could make an estimate of the population in the final year of the *desired* per capita consumption of different products. The expression 'desired per capita consumption' in practice requires to be spelled out in great detail. For one thing, who determines what is desired and under what conditions, e.g. price-income configurations? If we take into account desires of different individuals, we have to bring in income-distribution as an additional important factor. The problem of knowing individuals' preference maps may be sidetracked partly by extrapolating from time series data or by utilizing the cross-section information available. However, there is an essential circularity in setting the terminal levels of consumption for those items for which consumption is itself dependent on the level of income. If a rigid connection were to be maintained between consumption and income, setting the level of the former would be equivalent to setting the terminal level of income. If the connection is not so rigid, some policy is implied to control the target consumption. In consistency models in which the terminal bill of goods is a consequence of the stipulation of the other three sets of choice elements, this type of problem in setting consumption targets does not exist. In the present 'target' version of the consistency model a simple interpretation can be adopted of a planner setting a mix of products which satisfy certain minimums of nutrition, housing, and so on.

An estimate of consumption alone is going to be inadequate as a specification of the desired terminal bill of goods, even putting aside Government consumption and exports. We are, after all, interested in ensuring growth beyond the terminal year. As a first approximation let us make the provisional assumption that we want consumption of each type to be able to grow at *r* per cent per annum beyond the terminal year. This assumption of equiproportional growth as referring to the distant future has a considerable amount of analytical convenience. The levels of output in the different sectors in the terminal year may be easily calculated once the information on the rate of growth is available together with the likely values of structural coefficients.

We have the following balance equations:

H   113

$$X_i(t) = \sum_j X_{ij}(T) + \sum_j I_{ij}(T) + C_i(T) \tag{1}$$

$$\text{For, } t = T, \; X_i(T) = \sum_j a_{ij}X_j(T) + \sum_j b_{ij}\dot{X}_j(t) + C_i e^{rT}. \tag{2}$$

Our purpose now is to find a particular solution of this system of differential equations such that the X's are growing at the same rate as $C(t)$. In other words, we want to find a vector M such that $X = Me^{rt}$ is a solution of (2). This is easily done by writing

$$M_i e^{rT} = \sum_j a_{ij}M_j e^{rT} + \sum_j b_{ij}rM_j e^{rT} + C_i e^{rT}; \tag{3}$$

$$\text{or } M_i = \sum_j a_{ij}M_j + r\sum_j b_{ij}M_j + C_i; \tag{4}$$

after dividing both sides by e^{rT};

$$\text{or } M = AM + r\,BM + C$$
$$\text{or } (I - A - rB)\,M = C.$$
$$\text{Thus } M = (I - A - rB)^{-1}C.[1] \tag{5}$$

M has meaningful solutions if $(I - A - rB)^{-1}$ exists and contains non-negative elements. Since $(A + rB)$ is a non-negative square matrix, this condition will be satisfied if $\sum_j (a_{j1} + rb_{j1}) < 1$ for all i. Since r will normally be a small number, we can expect that in general, condition (6) will be satisfied. In fact an upper bound on r may be computed from this condition.

The main advantage of the assumption of equiproportional growth is that we get a vector equation for M which is entirely independent of 't'. This implies that if M's are chosen to satisfy the simple static condition of compatibility the growth of the economy at r per cent per annum is ensured for all $t \geq T$.

The assumption of equiproportional growth beyond the terminal year is introduced here as a purely auxiliary device. The very nature of the planning problem requires that we must impose some end conditions to ensure a determinate solution. Thus, if the concept of equiproportional growth is held to be economically uninteresting, there is nothing that prevents us from considering non-proportional growth. Naturally we do not

---

[1] One obtains the same time-free expression between M and C if the analysis proceeds in terms of discrete time units, which can be shown by reworking it in terms of difference equations.

expect the same degree of simplicity to characterize the non-proportional case. In fact we would not get a simple time-independent restriction on M's because e^{rT} cannot be cancelled from both sides. This may be shown by means of algebraic reasoning.

However, we can incorporate non-proportionality in growth rates for one time period beyond the terminal data. This ensures the really crucial condition that not all the capital will be eaten up at the terminal date and that some explicit provision is made for growth to continue into the future. All that we actually require is that growth should be continued for one post-terminal period, and then new long-term plans may be set up.

Let the demand for various consumption items, in particular the ith item, be represented by the simple expression $C_i(1+r_i)^{t-T}$ for $t \geq T$.[1] Now we want to ensure that at least for $t = (T, T+1)$ the above equation holds. For $t = T$, this is equal to C_1. At $t = T+1$, the demand is $C_1(1+r_1)$. Hence $\Delta C_1 = rC_1$. Now we have from the balance equation, $X_i = \Sigma_j a_{ij}X_j + \Sigma b_{ij}\Delta X_j + C_i$

for all X's. Then the following incremental relationship must hold:

$$\Delta X_i = \Sigma_j a_{ij}\Delta X_j + \Sigma b_{ij}\Delta^2 X_j + \Delta C_i. \tag{6}$$

If we ignore $\Delta^2 X_j$ as being of the second order of smallness,[2] we may write

$$\Delta X_i = \Sigma_j a_{ij}\Delta X_j + \Delta C_i.$$

Thus, $\Delta X = (I-A)^{-1}\Delta C.$ (7)

ΔK is then related to ΔX by the relation $\Delta K = b\Delta X$ where b is the matrix $[b_1 \ldots b_n]$. We write in more detail, $\Delta K_1 = b(I-A)^{-1}\Delta C_1$. Thus, if ΔC_1 is prescribed from outside, ΔK_1 is known. Once K_1 is known, we can determine the vector of output requirements at $t = T$ by using the simple relationship $X(T) = (I-A)^{-1}\{C_1(T) + \Delta K_1(T)\}$. In this way we can incorporate non-proportionality for the time period $(T, T+1)$.

The above discussion indicates one particular way of describ-

[1] It is more appropriate to use discrete time units in this connection.
[2] This amounts to ignoring the special side effects, if any, which may arise due to the acceleration or deceleration of the rate of growth in the post-terminal period as compared to the terminal period.

ing the terminal state. The advantage of the particular procedures briefly discussed is that specification of a single number 'r', or a vector (r) denoting growth beyond the terminal year, is enough, together with the structural information, to give us a vector of terminal stock requirements. By varying these magnitudes we may easily trace out the sensitiveness of the time path of the variables in which we are interested.

4. The model

Having described the initial and terminal conditions in some detail, we may now describe the manner in which the model is constructed in order to permit its solution when the intermediate rates of growth of consumption as well as the planning period are specified. This solution will indicate the use of the available resources to produce consumption and capital goods in the initial and subsequent periods. There are two sets of structural coefficients which must be known: current input-output and capital-output ratios.

We consider two sub-cases:

(i) *Equal rates of growth of consumption for* $t < T$

$X(t) = AX(t) + I(t) + C(t)$. Here A is the usual Leontief matrix of current input-output coefficients, $I(t)$ is the vector of investment goods delivered by sectors, $C(t)$ is the vector of consumption.

From the balance equation we get $(I - A) X(t) = I(t) + C(t)$, or $(I - A) X(t) = B\dot{X}(t) + C(t)$ where (B) is the matrix of intersectoral capital coefficients, $\dot{X}(t)$ represents the rate of change of X at 't'. Hence $X(t) = (I - A)^{-1} B \dot{X}(t) + (I - A)^{-1} C(t)$.

Let us now assume that $C(t) = Ce^{\rho t}$ where C represents the vector of initial consumption levels and ρ is the common exogenous rate at which consumption of various items is allowed to rise.

The solution to the differential equation written above has two parts. The first is obtained by solving the homogeneous equation: $X(t) = \{(I - A)^{-1}B\}\dot{X}(t)$. This has the solution $X(t) = Pe^{NT}$ where $N = 1/M$ and $M = \{(I - A)^{-1}B\}$. The concept of a matrix exponential is always well defined for a constant matrix; P is a vector to be determined with the help of initial conditions.

For the non-homogeneous part we derive the particular solution in the following way:

116

Put $X(t) = Qe^{\rho t}$ where Q is a set of unknowns to be determined and ρ is the rate of growth of consumption. Substituting $Qe^{\rho t}$ in the differential equation, we get

$$Qe^{\rho t} - M\rho Qe^{\rho t} = (I-A)^{-1}Ce^{\rho t}. \tag{8}$$

$e^{\rho t}$ cancels out. Thus we have

$$Q - M\rho Q = (I-A)^{-1}C. \tag{9}$$

Since ρ is just a scalar, we can write the above equation as

$$Q - \rho MQ = (I-A)^{-1}C. \tag{10}$$

Hence

$$(I - \rho M)Q = (I-A)^{-1}C \tag{11}$$

and

$$Q = (I-A)^{-1}C/(I-\rho M). \tag{12}$$

The complete solution for $X(t)$ may now be written as follows:

$$K(t) = Pe^{NT} + \{(I-A)^{-1}C/(I-\rho M)\}e^{\rho t} \tag{13}$$

$(I - \rho M)$ has a non-negative inverse because ρM is a non-negative square matrix with a maximum characteristic root less than 1.[1] To determine P and C we need information regarding initial and terminal states. We have n initial $X(o)$'s and terminal $X(T)$'s. Thus we have 2n equations to determine 2n unknowns, P's and C's.

Once $X(t)$ is determined, $K(t)$ is known. Therefore $\dot{K}(t)$, the pattern of accumulation, is also determined.

(ii) *Unequal rates of growth of consumption for* $t < T$

$C(t)$ can no longer be written as $Ce^{\rho t}$ since different components of consumption grow at different rates. The method of solution described above breaks down for this more general case. The use of matrix exponentials, however, enables us to write out the solution for this general case with relative ease.

Our general non-homogeneous equation is

$$X(t) = (I-A)^{-1}B\dot{X}(t) + C(t)$$

where

$$C(t) = \left\{ \begin{array}{c} C_1(t) \\ \cdot \\ \cdot \\ \cdot \\ C_n(t) \end{array} \right\} = \left\{ \begin{array}{c} C_1e^{\rho_1 t} \\ \cdot \\ \cdot \\ \cdot \\ C_ne^{\rho_n t} \end{array} \right\}$$

[1] This helps in computing an upper bound on the permissible ρ, i.e. a value of ρ such that $(I-\rho M)$ has a non-negative inverse.

117

or

$$\dot{X}(t) = \{(I-A)^{-1}B\}^{-1}X(t) - \{(I-A)^{-1}B\}^{-1}C(t) \tag{14}$$

which can be written as

$$\dot{X}(t) = NX(t) + f(t),$$

where

$$N = \{(I-A)^{-1}B\}^{-1} \text{ and } f(t) = \{-(I-A)^{-1}B\}C(t).$$

Noting

$$\frac{d}{dt}[e^{-Nt}X(t)]e^{-Nt}[\dot{X}(t) - NX(t)] = e^{-Nt}f(t). \tag{15}$$

Hence

$$e^{-Nt}X(t) = P + \int_0^t e^{-Nt}f(t)dt.$$

Or

$$X(t) = e^{Nt}P + \int_0^t e^{-Nt}f(t)dt.^1 \tag{16}$$

Since $X(t)$ and $f(t)$ are known functions, the equation for $X(t)$, with the integrations performed, are functions of P, t and $f(t)$. Since $f(t)$ is in turn a function of C's and ρ's, $X(t)$ is a function of P's, C's, ρ's and t. ρ's are given data. P's and C's are determined with the help of initial and terminal conditions. Thus for the more general case the same qualitative results can be obtained even though the technique of solution differs somewhat.

The presence of gestation lags in the economic system makes a difference equation formulation of the model a more appropriate one for situations where such lags are important in relation to the length of the planning period.

The balance equation $X(t) = AX(t) + I(t) + C(t)$ would be the same in the difference equation version as in the differential equation form. However, we cannot write $I(t) = B\dot{X}(t)$ when there is a significant gestation lag in the system. In fact if the length of the gestation period is assumed to be uniform and equal to g years then $I(t) = \dfrac{B}{g}[X(t+g) - X(t)],$ (17)

---

[1] See R. Bellman, *Stability Theory of Differential Equations*, New York, 1953.

if capacity is assumed to be built up uniformly over the interval 'o' to 'g'. Thus we have

$$X(t) = AX(t) + \frac{B}{g}[X(t+g) - X(t)] + C(t). \tag{18}$$

The homogeneous part is now a system of difference equations of order g. With the help of matrix notation, we are treating it as if it were one matrix system of order g. Now this solution has one dominant root. This may be easily demonstrated. The solution corresponding to the dominant root is written as follows:

$$X(t) = P\left(g\sqrt{\frac{g(I-A) + B/g}{B}}\right)^t \text{ where P is to be determined}$$

from initial conditions. The gth root of $g\sqrt{\dfrac{g(I-A) + B/g}{B}}$ is well

defined for $g \geq 0$.[1]

We have now to determine a solution for the non-homogeneous part. We have the following relationship:

$$(I-A)X = \frac{B}{g}[X(t+g) - X(t)] + Q(1+r)^t; \tag{19}$$

or

$$(I-A+\frac{B}{g})X(t) = \frac{B}{g}X(t+g) + Q(1+r)^t \tag{20}$$

Now try a solution for $X(t) = X(1+r)^t$ where r is the rate at which exogenous consumption is increasing.
Cancelling out $(1+r)^t$, we get

$$(I-A+\frac{B}{g})\underline{X} = \frac{B}{g}\underline{X}(1+r)^g + Q; \tag{21}$$

---

[1] Strictly speaking the above procedure yields a valid solution only if we assume a special initial condition to prevail right from the start. Otherwise we are justified in ignoring the other components of the general solution corresponding to the non-dominant roots only if interest is concentrated on the long-run solution. For short periods this procedure breaks down. It is then necessary to postulate 'g' sets of initial conditions. Together with the open ends pertaining to consumption there will be $(g+1)$ sets of constants to be determined. Information on the terminal sets of X's together with the information on g sets of X's pertaining to $X(0), X(-1), \ldots, X(g-1)$ permit the determination of all the constants of the problem.

119

or

$$\left\{ I - A + \frac{B}{g} - \frac{B}{g}(1+r)^g \right\}_- = Q; \tag{22}$$

or

$$\underline{X} = \frac{Q}{I - A + \frac{B}{g} - \frac{B}{g}(1+r)^g} \tag{23}$$

We can write the complete solution as:

$$X(t) = P\left[g\sqrt{g\frac{(I-A+B/g)}{B}} \right]^t +$$

$$\frac{Q}{\left\{ I - A + \frac{B}{g} - \frac{B}{g}(1+r)^g \right\}(1+r)^t} \tag{24}$$

For the interesting case where $g=1$ we get

$$X(t) = P\frac{(I-A+B)^t}{A} + \frac{Q}{I-A-rB}(1+r)^t \tag{25}$$

Since we know $X(0)$ and $X(T)$ we have $2n$ equations to determine $2n$ unknowns P & Q. Thus the discussion is complete for the case of gestation lags with an average length equal to g.

If we have different gestation lags in different sectors, then the formal manipulation of the model will have to be along somewhat different lines, but the essential point remains unchanged.[1]

5. *Interpretation of the model*
The analysis given in Section 4 shows quite clearly that the one-sector model is capable of being extended to a multi-sector case in a straightforward fashion. The qualitatively interesting point that arises in the multi-sector model is the possibility of non-proportional growth. This has naturally no analogue in the one-sector model. Further, the determination of the terminal state is a tricky business. Apart from that, all we have done is just multiply the number of variables, but the use of matrix exponential keeps the notation perspicacious. In fact

---

[1] The use of difference equations in multi-sectoral models with lags playing an important part is discussed in great detail in Chapters IV–VI of *The Logic of Investment Planning* by S. Chakravarty, North Holland Publishing Company, Amsterdam. The discussion there is primarily from the point of view of numerical extrapolation, a method of solution particularly suited to situations characterized by significant differences in the lengths of sectoral gestation lags.

it is the use of matrix methods which shows the similarity with the one-sector case so clearly.

However, there is a source of complication in the many-sector model which relates not to mathematical consistency of the dynamic model, which is obviously satisfied here. The doubt arises as to whether we would preserve non-negativity of all the variables. An analysis of the solution of the differential equation shows that there exists an initial configuration for which the system possesses a solution which has all non-negative components. Thus there is no necessary contradiction between the model and the requirement of non-negativity. But the real question is whether for any arbitrary set of initial conditions we shall necessarily preserve non-negativity in all the variables for all future periods.

A closer look at the form of the solution will enable us to clarify the question considerably. We write the solution for $X(t)$ in the following way:

$$X(t) = Pg^{Nt} + \frac{C'}{I - \rho M} \rho t. \tag{26}$$

This is the solution that corresponds to the continuous case. The matrix N is actually a composite one and may be written explicitly as follows:

$$N = \{(I - A)^{-1} B\}^{-1}$$

Now if we ignore for the time being the non-homogeneous part, then $X(t)$ will preserve non-negativity for arbitrary non-negative initial conditions if N is a non-negative matrix. In fact it can be shown to be a sufficient condition.

A necessary and sufficient condition on the matrix N which ensures non-negativity of solutions for all $t > 0$ is the following: if for any given matrix N we can find a scalar c such that the matrix $cI + N$, where I is the identity matrix and is non-negative, then the matrix exponential e^{Nt} is also non-negative.[1] A different way of stating this condition is the following: e^{Nt} is non-negative if and only if the matrix $N = (a_{ij})$ is such that $a_{ij} > 0$ for $i \neq j$. This leaves the sign of the diagonal elements entirely open.

---

[1] To show this write $e^{At} = e^{(cI+A)t} \cdot e^{-cIt}$. Now $e^{(cI+A)t}$ is non-negative because $cI + A$ is non-negative. e^{-cIt}, being a scalar exponential, is necessarily non-negative. Since the product of two non-negative matrices is non-negative, e^{At} is clearly non-negative. See R. Bellman, *Introduction to Matrix Analysis.*

As the inverse of a non-negative matrix, N will have mixed signs, but we cannot say offhand if the negative signs apply only to the diagonal elements. The initial conditions are assumed to be non-negative.

In extending the discussion to the non-homogeneous case an interesting possibility arises. In equation (26) if ρ is such that modulus $(\rho M) < 1$, then $\dfrac{1}{I-\rho M}$ has a non-negative inverse and has therefore a matrix multiplier expansion, e.g. $I+\rho M+(\rho M)^2 + \ldots$ etc. If C′ is also non-negative, then $(C'/I-\rho M)e^{\rho t}$ is a non-negative expression. In other words, the non-homogeneous system has one characteristic positive root ρ and a characteristic vector associated with it which is positive. This positive root is additional to the positive root which the homogeneous system contains.[1] It follows that we may have a value of ρ which is greater in absolute value than any other root and therefore dominates all of them. The existence of this additional root in the non-homogeneous case will help to maintain non-negativity conditions for a finite time period.

The economic implication of this argument is that if we have final demand expanding at a fast enough rate for all the commodities in question, then negative output levels cannot arise. This is true because decumulation can arise only if some sectors are contracting while others are expanding. Since contraction is ruled out, the possibility of capital stocks and output levels turning out to be negative is also eliminated. By generalizing the argument to the case where the different sectors are growing at unequal rates it would be possible to show that the conclusion on non-negativity retains its validity although the derivation of the necessary and sufficient condition will be more difficult.

From the point of view of preserving non-negativity it would appear to be a good thing if ρ were made very large. This would increase the probability that ρ would dominate all other roots. However, given the technology and the initial and terminal conditions, a very high ρ may not be feasible. Infeasibility of a stipulated ρ would show itself in rendering C′ negative while

---

[1] By virtue of Frobenius's assumptions on the matrix M.

122

the argument of the preceding paragraphs depends on C' being positive.[1]

In a developing economy there is nothing in the logic of things to prevent certain sectors from declining absolutely, e.g. the case of inferior goods when income expands or the decline in production for export when a primary producing country turns to a concentration on industrialization. However, in the case of countries like India, in which per capita income is quite low, only a very substantial increase in the level of income or a very fine commodity classification would give the inferior good problem any importance. Moreover, for balance of payments purposes, production of primary commodities will have to be expanded for some time to come in most of the less-developed countries.

There is also the possibility of changing from any arbitrary set of initial conditions to a special initial configuration which would preserve non-negativity of all output levels. In this case the planning problem is broken into two phases: (a) the preliminary one of getting to these special proportions and (b) the problem of moving from this special position to the desired terminal situation.

5.1. *Singularity of the B Matrix*

If the B-matrix is singular, then we cannot use the method of solution outlined in previous sections. Instead we try a different technique of solution. Our fundamental equation is as follows:

$$(I-A)X(t) = B\frac{dx}{dt} \tag{27}$$

Now try a solution $X(t) = Me^{\lambda t}$. Substituting this relation in the previous equation, we get

$$(I-A)Me^{\lambda t} = \lambda BM\, e^{\lambda t}. \tag{28}$$

Since $e^{\lambda t}$ may be cancelled out, we thus have the following equation:

$$(I-A-\lambda B)M = e. \tag{29}$$

For non-trivial solutions to exist, $|\ I-A-\lambda B\ | = 0$.

This gives us the characteristic polynomial in λ. This is degree 'n'. We have thus 'n' roots. We get corresponding values of X.

[1] This argument is again valid for a finite time horizon.

These are determined up to a scale factor. Using some normalizing device, we can determine them uniquely.

Our solution for X(t) can now be written as

$$X(t) = \sum_j C_j M_{ij} e^{\lambda_j t}. \tag{30}$$

The C_j's are determined with the help of initial conditions.

The above method of solution does not depend on the non-singularity of the B-matrix.[1]

5.2. *The variability of the input coefficients*

The entire analysis has proceeded on the assumption of constancy of input-output and capital-output coefficients. This may be easily criticized as being unduly restrictive. There are some ways in which the limitations of these assumptions may be somewhat relaxed. One partial relaxation would come through making input-output dependence linear rather than proportional. Thus we write $X_{ij} = a_{ij}X_j + b_{ij}$ where $b_{ij} > 0$ or < 0. In the first case relative factor requirement diminishes, while in the other case it increases. We can consider the first situation as illustrating some aspects of the law of increasing returns, while the second would serve as an example of the operation of the law of diminishing returns. Our equation system is easily adapted to take into account this slightly generalized situation.

There is another way of considering this variability. This method is applicable when we are working out iterative solutions to our system of equations. We reduce for computational purposes the differential equations to the corresponding set of finite difference equations. Then in working out solutions we use changing sets of coefficients depending on the levels of output already attained. This is a rather effective method of taking into account variability of coefficients and often corresponds to the way a planner adjusts his production targets through successive approximations.

II. EXTENSION TO AN OPEN ECONOMY

The previous discussion has been in terms of a closed economy: there was no demand on resources for production for export and no availability of resources for filling the final bill of

[1] However, singularity of the B-matrix would indicate that the solution is unique only for properly chosen subsets of the original set of variables.

goods except from domestic production. No questions arose of import substitution, export drives, or balance of payments restrictions. But for an open economy these questions do arise and can and must be taken into account.

Importing a commodity and producing it at home may be regarded as alternative activities for some sectors, while noncompetitive imports may be treated as a primary factor whose availability is restricted by the foreign exchange constraint. This approach cannot be introduced into the framework of the model itself because analysis of a dynamic model with 'built-in' substitution possibilities is beyond our immediate scope. On the other hand, a static model, even with substitution possibilities, would ignore a range of significant factors connected with planning for development over time.

For projecting export demand by different sectors nothing better is suggested here than the usual projection techniques based on price elasticities. The significance of alternative projections and the use of resources to achieve them can then be investigated by use of the model.

Imports take the place of domestic production, but in a developing economy it would be a mistake to consider the dependence on imports as constant over time. Yet the degree of dependence is to some extent a matter of choice, the consequences of which require analysis. The alternatives from which choices can be made have to be generated outside the model which, as for exports, can then be used to investigate their implications. The following general approach may be used for this purpose. With an aggregate projection of imports and a forecast of foreign assistance availabilities, the amount and phasing of the foreign exchange restriction can be established. The problem is then to allocate the total among various commodities. If the timing of foreign assistance is flexible, determination of the best timing is an additional problem. An allocation among sectors and over time has to be made on bases exogenous to the formal planning model itself. The solution can then be computed and the results examined and compared with results obtained from an alternative allocation.

The balance equation for an open economy is:
$X(t)=AX(t)+B\dot{X}(t)+C(t)+E(t)-M(t)$, where $E(t)$ is the vector of exports, $M(t)$ the vector of competitive imports, and

125

all the other symbols have their usual meanings. Non-competitive imports are ignored or included in $M(t)$. If non-competitive imports are kept outside the model, they may be brought into the picture when total export earnings are being compared with the total import requirements. An alternative procedure would be to consider non-competitive imports as constituting 'empty sectors'. For such empty sectors, $X(t)=0$, implying that domestic availability is zero, and $E(t)=0$ unless re-exports are allowed. They may be used to augment capacity elsewhere in the economy or to supply raw materials or for final consumption.

For sectors $1, \ldots, n$ in which domestic production takes place
$$X(t)+M(t)=A\ X(t)+B\dot{X}(t)+C(t)+E(t).$$
If $M(t)=\lambda X(t)$, where λ is a diagonal matrix $\begin{bmatrix} \lambda_1 & & \\ & \cdot & \\ & & \cdot \ \lambda_n \end{bmatrix}$

indicating the ratio of competitive imports per unit of domestic production,
$$(I+\lambda-A)\ X(t)=B\ \dot{X}(t)+C(t)+E(t).$$
Let $C(t)=Ce^{\rho t}$ and $E(t)=Ee^{\mu t}$ as a first approximation. This augmented system has the following solution:

$$X(t)=Pe^{N't}+\frac{(I+\lambda-A)^{-1}Ce^{\rho t}}{I-\rho M'}+\frac{(I+\lambda-A^{-1}Ee^{\mu t})}{I-\mu M^1}$$

where $N'=\dfrac{1}{M'}$ and $M'=[(I+\lambda-A)^{-1}B]^{-1}$. There are now three sets of constants to determine the P's, C's, and E's, but only two sets of equations involving the initial and terminal conditions, the $X(0)$'s and the $X(T)$'s. This leaves, therefore, n degrees of freedom. Any n values can then be assumed on an arbitrary basis. For example, all C's may be chosen arbitrarily or all E's. However, such exclusive choices will often be unrealistic. There are many mixed choices possible consisting partly of E's and C's. Thus the introduction of foreign trade increases the number of degrees of freedom substantially.

Once X's are known, $M=M'+M''$, where M' and M'' stand for competitive and non-competitive imports respectively, may be easily calculated. This total may be compared with the total of export earnings. If there is a deficit on the balance of payments, this may be either met by foreign assistance or by import substitution. The nature and extent of import substitution may be determined from the model by changing λ's or by deciding to fill up 'empty sectors'. The total effectiveness of import substitution in any direction may be determined by computing appropriately changed inverses of $(I+\lambda-A)$ matrices. In this way the main consistency problems that arise in planning in an open economy may be taken into account.

8

A SIMPLE OPTIMIZING PLANNING MODEL

LOUIS LEFEBER

This chapter, as those of Chakravarty and Eckaus, intends to suggest that national economic planning can be reinforced by the use of rational planning models.[1] The model is not offered as a contribution to economic theory. Rather it is an effort to adapt the tools of modern economic analysis to problems of planning. Here a note of caution must be sounded. Even the most advanced methods of modern theory cannot be expected to throw light on all details of a development programme. The current state of computational skills and electronic capacity, moreover, cannot cope with numerical solutions of non-homogeneous systems which simultaneously deal with a meaningful number of sectors. At this stage rational planning models must therefore be viewed and understood as skeleton approximations, the purpose of which is to reveal major interrelationships within the economy.

Furthermore, in the absence of knowing *all* the pertinent relationships over a relevant horizon and in the absence of exactly specified social or planner's preferences ('the social welfare function'), rational schemes themselves cannot yield a national plan; i.e. they are indeterminate. They can provide alternative paths to economic growth, all of which may be in some sense efficient, but they do not provide a method for choosing the optimal alternative. The selection of the path must be done by careful consideration of what is acceptable to and desirable for society. Even if a concrete social welfare function is not known, approximations to it—as a whole or in

---

[1] The chapter is based on an 'Internal Research Memorandum' prepared by the author in the autumn of 1960 while in India as a member of the CENIS India research group. The memorandum was motivated by the evident need for more exact or rational methods of planning than those used in the preparation of the Third Five Year Plan. The kinship between the model presented in this chapter and the model of Chapter 6 should be evident. The present version of this chapter benefited from the comments of Professor R. S. Eckaus.

parts—will be attempted by the policy-maker. They may be dictatorially postulated; they are more likely, however, to be rooted in the political process, in historical and international cross-section observation; and the intuition of the policy-maker necessarily also plays an important role.

Considered in this light, i.e. from the pragmatic point of view of selecting a path, there is no earth-shaking difference between optimizing and consistency models. Any efficient path obtained through mathematical optimization must by definition be a consistent path (though the converse does not necessarily hold true). But because there is no readily available, and well specified, social welfare function to determine the optimum path, a choice has to be made from an infinite number of paths by some other criteria.

Consistency models of the type Chakravarty and Eckaus are discussing can be used to answer the following question: given initial economic conditions, terminal capacities and consumptions, is there a feasible path which can connect the two? If there is none—or if the path does not satisfy certain side conditions, such as minimum consumption levels—alternative terminal consumption and capacity targets must be searched for. An optimizing model, on the other hand, can avoid searching for terminal targets consistent with initial conditions if the feasibility surface (or relevant portions thereof) for all choice variables can be mapped. Here, however, is exactly the problem. The mapping of the surface requires the variation of arbitrary weights for all final outputs—and for the terminal capacities—which can turn into a staggering combinatorial problem if the numbers of sectors are large. Hence, at least at the current state of the art, great restraint is required in the use of the weights.

The number of arbitrary weights can be reduced by trading on the mathematical superiority of an optimizing model. By not treating terminal capacities as variables but as predetermined constants, the corresponding weights can be eliminated. Further economy can be achieved by keeping only some consumer goods in the maximand and requiring others to conform to stipulated minimum requirements. The most promising simplification consists of introducing a single consumption activity for each period based on fixed consumption coefficients (i.e. composite goods).

The selection of terminal capacities involves more than the relatively simple question of staying within the boundaries of feasibility. It is primarily a value judgment concerning the needs of society beyond the terminal date. Hence under these conditions value judgments have to be exercised in two steps: first, when we select the terminal targets, and second, when we choose the path to attain them.

With this operation some of the attractiveness of optimizing models is lost since the experimental process of selecting feasible and desirable terminal conditions can be just as painful as in the case of consistency models. The optimizing model still has a very appealing feature—that of preserving a range of choice (degrees of freedom) for any feasible set of terminal capacities. Hence portions of the feasibility surface—alternative paths—can be 'felt out' just by playing on the keyboard of arbitrary weights. Whether this advantage is significant depends on the computational difficulties of optimizing versus consistency models. Only actual experimentation will tell.

The framework of the present model is dictated by computational and statistical feasibility rather than analytical sophistication. Furthermore, it is only one of many approaches, all of which may be feasible and some of which may have more desirable properties. Again, the most satisfactory construct, one which is both computationally feasible and relevant in its assumptions, will be obtained only through actual experimentation.

The maximand of an m sector model for n time periods is given by the following relationship:

$$\sum_{t=1}^{m} \sum_{i=1}^{n} W^i(t) X_c^i(t) \tag{1}$$

In accordance with the foregoing discussion only consumer goods of different time periods are contained in it. These are denoted by the $X_c^i(t)$; the W—s are arbitrary weights.

The constraints of the model are given by equations (2) to (11). In addition, the variables must be non-negative.[1]

---

[1] Also certain Hawkins-Simon type conditions must be satisfied which in this context we shall take for granted. And, of course, the coefficients of the variables must be linearly independent and the system must be consistent for a unique solution.

The distribution and origin of any one output is summarized as follows:

$$X_c^i(t) + \sum_{j=1}^{m} X_{kj}^i(t) + \sum_{j=1}^{m} X_{Ij}^i(t) + X_x^i(t) - X_M^i(t) - X^i(t) \leqq 0; \qquad (2)$$

The two negative terms, X^i and X_M^i, denote the domestic production and import of a given good, respectively. The sum total of these is distributed into consumption (X_c^i), addition to capacity in diverse sectors (X_{jk}^i), flow into the production of or intermediate use in diverse sectors (X_{Ij}^i), and finally exports (X_x^i). A good which is imported cannot also be exported; hence, either X_x^i or X_M^i (or both) must be zero. Which is to vanish is determined by the balance relationship (9) as well as the other constraints of the system.

If in order to economize on the number of arbitrary weights we want to reduce the number of variables entering the objective function, some of the X_c^i—s can be held at a constant level in (2) and the corresponding weights in (1) can be replaced by zero. The consumption levels for these items can be determined for each time period by the application of outside criteria based on population growth and expected income-consumption relationships. This procedure of course requires an initial expectation of income growth and distribution. The independent projection of this growth, however, is necessitated anyway by the need to set reasonable terminal capacity conditions. More difficult is the strategic question: which consumptions should be retained as variables and which should be fixed? One could certainly argue that one should fix those items whose statistical predictability involves the smallest risk. These would be primarily goods of low income and price elasticity. On the other hand, these are also the goods which in a country like India make up the overwhelming level of consumption, and their exclusion from the objective function may significantly narrow the range of feasible paths. Again, only careful consideration and actual experimentation will throw light on the projection's sensitivity to these choices.

An alternative and from the computational point of view rather promising way of formulating the maximand is in terms of consumption activities. For this purpose we define a variable

131

C(t) denoting market basket for total consumption in each time period. C(t) should be conceived of as a composite good made up of the different $X^i_c(t)$ in fixed proportion. Hence,

$$C(t) = \min\left\{\frac{X^1_c(t),}{c^1} \cdot \cdots \cdots \cdot, \frac{X^m_c(t)}{c^m}\right\}$$

where c^i, which also can vary from period to period, denotes the fixed consumption coefficients. For each good entering C(t) a relationship $c^i C(t) \leq x^i_c(t)$ must be added to the system. With the exception of the maximand, all other relationships from 2 to 11 remain the same.

The maximand itself will assume the following form:

$$\Sigma_t W(t) C(t).$$

Under these conditions the ratio $W(t) - W(t+1) : W(t+1)$ is nothing but the marginal rate of return over cost, or (in equilibrium) the market rate of interest between two adjacent periods. The number of variables which enter the maximand with a non-zero weight are reduced to the number of periods under consideration.

With this formulation the problem of selecting suitable sets of arbitrary weights as well as the difficulty of tracing out a relevant feasible surface is greatly diminished. First, we know that the weights corresponding to later years can never exceed the weights of earlier years. Second, the greater the terminal stock requirements relative to initial savings, the greater must be the rate of interest needed to bring about the desired stock. Third, the prevailing marginal rate of return can be independently estimated for the economy. These three pieces of advance information will not, in themselves, give us the exact weights to be used; however, they can provide the basis for starting with a plausible set. Once a solution with plausible weights is obtained, theoretical insights concerning the relationship between interest and consumption should help us to derive the relevant portions of the feasibility surface. Of course, the advantage of an easily manageable weight system can be attained only at the cost of exogenously estimating market baskets (i.e. fixed consumption coefficients) for each time period.

The production relationships are described by the following two functions:

$$a_i^h X^i(t) = X_{1i}^h(t) \leqq 0; \tag{3}$$

$$a_k^i X^i(t) = KS^i(t) \leqq 0; \tag{4}$$

Expression (3) describes the intermediate use of produced factors in the production of the i-th output, a_i^h being the Leontief flow coefficient. Function (4) expresses the use of capacity (capital) in the production of the i-th good with a_k^i as a capital coefficient. KS^i denotes the existing capacity for the production of the i-th good. Technological change is not endogenously built into the model. The coefficients can be exogenously adopted for each time period according to one's judgment (forecast) of expected technological change. Alternatively, at the cost of introducing more relationships (and with due care to avoid upsetting the first order homogeneity of the system), technical change can be made endogenous. In processes where evidently more than one fixed coefficient technology exists more than one production function can be introduced, leaving to the system itself to select the most appropriate technology. This may be important in areas where new investment could be based on completely different capacity requirements.

The relationships (5) to (9) indicate the availability and accumulation of capacity in the different sectors. KS^i is capital stock or capacity in the i-th sector, and K^i indicates the current addition to existing capacity—i.e. gross investment in the i-th sector. d^i is a depreciation coefficient. The relationships are as follows:

$$KS^i(t+1) - K^i(t-g) + d^i KS^i(t) - KS^i(t) \leqq 0; \tag{5}$$

$$b_j^i K(t) - X_{kj}^h(t) \leqq 0; \tag{6}$$

$$KS^i(1) = \overline{KS^i(1)}; \tag{7}$$

$$K^i(1-s) = \overline{K^i(1-s)}; \qquad s = 1, 2, \ldots g-1; \tag{8}$$

$$KS^i(n+v) = \overline{KS^i(n+v)} \qquad v = 1, 2, \ldots g. \tag{9}$$

The change in capacity due to net investment is described by (5). Lagged gross investment is added to and current depreciation is subtracted from capacity in time t to obtain capacity in the next period. As indicated, investment is assumed to become active only after some gestation period denoted by g.

133

The latter may be as much as four years in heavy industries, mining, transportation, and certain power projects. At the same time, even in these industries much of the investment may have no significant gestation periods, e.g. replacement and additions to existing facilities. Hence, in order to avoid meaningless averaging, it may be necessary to separate 'heavy' from 'light' capacity and/or to arbitrarily introduce more than one technology. The cost is of course an increase in variables as well as relationships. On the other hand, if the unit period of the model is made up of more than one year, the lag itself gets partially or totally absorbed within the period, and the problem may disappear. For instance, if we choose the year 2000 A.D. as our terminal date and our unit periods are five years, no lag would have to be introduced in most sectors. There is of course always a residual ambiguity about the contribution to production of new investment, in its first active period, because from the model's point of view a time period is a point in time, whereas in reality it is a time span.

The flow of resources into capacity creation is described by relationship (6), where b_j^i is the flow coefficient of outputs into investment. (7) represents the initial conditions which are defined by the observed current capacities at the beginning of the planning periods. However, as indicated by (8), capacity additions created in previous periods—predetermined for the model— become active during the first g periods.

(9) Shows the terminal conditions, not only for the terminal year itself but also for all subsequent years over the duration of the investment lag. Since we have removed the terminal capacities from the maximand, they must be set exogenously by methods which are described, for example, in the papers of Chakravarty and Eckaus and do not have to be discussed here. It is useful to point out, however, that the longer the planning horizon of the model, the greater flexibility exists in the choice of paths.[1] As time itself progresses, the planning framework must be regularly recomputed, based on new technological information and initial conditions as well as with new terminal

[1] These comments refer to the strategy of making the best use of rational planning models, and not to the somewhat vague question of what is the relevant planning horizon for the policy-maker. With the usually high real interest rates prevailing in developing economies, the economic horizon and with it the present discounted value of the cost of distant errors shrinks rapidly with time.

conditions estimated in the light of most recent observations and criteria. Thus in a process of continuous planning the terminal conditions of any one planning framework are distant goals relevant only for the implementation of the initial planning period of each recomputed framework.

The last two relationships refer to the foreign trade sector of the economy:

$$\sum_i P_M^i X_M^i(t) - \sum_j P_x^j X_x^j(t) \leqq A; \tag{10}$$

$$X_x^j(t) \leqq \overline{X}_x^j(t). \tag{11}$$

(10) is a balance of payments equation indicating that the deficit on current account cannot exceed a given foreign balance (A), negative or positive (depending on the state of foreign aid, capital movements, etc.). The prices of input and export goods (P_M^i and P_x^i) are exogenously given in foreign exchange (say pounds sterling). The balance relationship incorporates infinitely elastic demand for exports and supply of imports. The assumption about the demand for exports is completely untenable in a country like India which supplies significant percentages of the world jute, tea, and certain other raw material markets. The unreality of the assumption is offset by relationship (11), which exogenously limits the exportable amounts for each sector. This constraint is needed not only to correct for the supply assumption (which could be done by more elegant ways) but also because the properties of a linear model could force full specialization in many sectors (analogously to the two-good, constant-cost trading model) way beyond what in reality is feasible. Without constraint (11), as an extreme case, the model might suggest that India should be turned into one gigantic tea plantation and import all consumer goods and the capital for terminal capacities. While constraining exports prevents the model from going to non-feasible extremes, it also requires an independent estimation of the country's export prospects. No such limitation has to be put on imports where the total expenditure is limited by export proceeds (and foreign aid incorporated in A). However, if domestic growth in a sector is jeopardized by imports, quotas can be established for infant protection exactly as for exports in expression (11).

The foreign trade sector completes the model. For any one

path there must be a corresponding set of shadow prices which sustain the equilibrium. The shadow prices, however, would seldom correspond to readily identifiable prices in reality since the sectors the model deals with are in most cases aggregates. The important exception is the shadow price attached to the balance of payments (relationship 10), which unambiguously refers to one single homogeneous scarce resource, i.e. foreign exchange, and which will presumably vary from period to period. Since the valuation of a proper exchange rate is crucial in planning, its estimation could be a significant bonus.

Much could be—and possibly should be—added to improve the model's reality. For instance, labour (even skilled labour) was neglected. Unskilled labour can be legitimately left out in the case of India, and the chosen path can be used as a basis for estimating skilled labour requirements. Alternatively, skilled labour groups can be directly included without conceptual problems. But one must remember that increasing effort to obtain closer and closer approximations to reality must sooner or later result in diminishing returns as each variable and relationship added for reality's sake is bound to increase the computational complexity of the system. How far can one go in approaching reality without too great a price, only extended experimentation will determine. But if computer technology and computational techniques continue to increase at the same rate as in the recent past, the approximation of reality can also be improved. In the meantime the already existing analytical tools and computational facilities could be combined into methods so superior to the impressionistic approaches to planning currently employed—which themselves do not seem to result in close approximations of reality—that nothing can be lost and much could be gained by a gradual increase in the use of rational frameworks of the general type presented above.

9

AN APPRAISAL OF
ALTERNATIVE PLANNING MODELS[1]

S. CHAKRAVARTY
R. S. ECKAUS

Certainly one of the most powerful incentives to the clarification of theoretical frameworks must be the potentiality of their application. Discussion of multi-sectoral, inter-temporal economic planning models in a particular context may not have led to a resolution of the conceptual problems, but it has provided a strong stimulus.

In this chapter we report some results of such stimulation. We attempt an appraisal of various types of consistency models, including the one discussed in the preceding paper, through an explicit comparison with planning models with optimization features. Our notions of what is involved in the use of fully optimizing models are based on the theoretical literature on this subject as well as our independent work and the suggestions of our colleagues.[2] As will become clear, we make different judgments as to the actual or potential availability of various types of empirical information. For the most part, except where on *a priori* grounds the strictly computational problems appear to preclude some particular theoretical formulation, we abstract from such problems.

Both the consistency models and the optimizing approach to planning entail a common framework of production involving many sectors with interconnecting flows. The conditions of production are those of the usual Leontief-type models and are described by two matrices: one of 'flow' coefficients for

[1] The authors are indebted to M. Andreatta and P. Sevaldson for stimulating discussions which were the origin of some of the points in this paper.

[2] See R. Dorfman, P. A. Samuelson and R. Solow, *Linear Programming and Economic Analysis*, 1958, especially Chapters 9 to 12; S. Chakravarty, 'Optimal Savings with Finite Planning Horizons', *International Economic Review*, September 1962; R. S. Eckaus and L. Lefeber, 'Capital Formation and Economic Growth: A Theoretical and Empirical Analysis', *Review of Economics and Statistics*, May 1962, and reproduced in the present volume.

current inputs, and one of 'capital' coefficients for additions to capacity. It is not necessary that these matrices be the same in every period, but in both types of the models they are specified exogenously and the models are not required to choose the most appropriate coefficients. It is possible to embody technological changes through variation of the flow and capital coefficients. This can be accomplished by making the input-output dependences linear rather than proportional, or when working out a solution by an iterative process to change the coefficients exogenously, perhaps depending on the level of output achieved. Thus 'fixed' coefficients are not a necessary feature of this type of planning framework. Technological change can be embodied in a similar way to the extent that it is known and put into effect. Outputs are divided among intermediate flows and final uses in private and government consumption, capital formation, and exports. For the purposes of this note we abstract from special considerations relating to exports and government consumption.

I. A CONSISTENCY MODEL

The intent of this approach as it has been formulated in the previous chapter is to decide if there exists and, if so, to determine for each year of the planning period a pattern of output and investment which is consistent with a particular 'target' vector of terminal production levels and specified rates of growth of consumption during the plan period. The 'free' variables which may adjust to permit the solution of the problem are the initial levels of consumption. The working of the system is constrained on the production side, however, by the specification of the initial levels of capacity in each sector and the conditions of production as described by the two Leontief matrices.

The whole object of the framework is to find an intertemporally consistent set of outputs, investments, and consumptions within the planning period. There is no presumption that the path so determined is an optimal one. Strictly speaking, the concept of an 'optimum path' cannot be defined within the limits of a single consistency model. It is, however, always possible to derive alternative consistent paths of development

138

by varying the targets and other exogenous conditions which are set. The planners may then choose the one particular consistent path which they consider most satisfactory. This mechanism of selection is not included within the model itself.

In the 'target' version of the consistency model the construction of the planning framework proceeds in the following way:

(1) The first step is to establish the terminal conditions; these are the targets to be achieved at the end of the planning period. Since the initial conditions are conveniently specified in terms of the full capacity levels of production prevailing at the beginning of the planning period, the terminal conditions are also set in the same dimensions. From the mathematical point of view it is only necessary that these conditions be in some way established, whether it be done by picking a set of numbers from a table of random digits or by a set of independent calculations. From an economic point of view there is unavoidably some arbitrariness in confining our forward vision in a planning model to, say, five or fifteen years and stating the goals to be achieved then without looking beyond. A method is suggested which at least makes explicit the nature of the arbitrary decisions which are involved, as they always are in any planning model with a finite horizon.

For the end of the planning period an independent estimate is made of target levels of consumption of each item. The method of estimation is left as an independent procedure at this stage of model building. Desired per capita levels of consumption of different items might be used with population projections. Or an aggregate annual average growth in per capita consumption can be projected and then divided among consumption items by a combination of Engel relations and stipulation based on exogenous considerations. Even when terminal consumption levels have been specified, that establishes only one of the target final 'bill-of-goods vectors', and by itself does not take account of the desire to have economic growth continuing beyond the planning period. In order to ensure this it can, for example, be specified that consumption of all items be able to grow at some particular rate, r, beyond the terminal year. Having already established the final consumption levels, the specification of a growth rate in consumption to be achieved beyond the final period permits the derivation of terminal production levels in each sector along the lines discussed in the previous paper.

The post-terminal evaluation guaranteed by this type of calculation is characterized by equiproportional growth in all consumption items. However, as demonstrated in the preceding chapter, it is possible to derive a set of conditions on the terminal capital stocks which will permit growth of consumption in specified non-proportional rates in the first post-terminal period.

Following the time path directed by the model up to and including the terminal period conditions derived as above will make possible further growth in the post-terminal period at rates which can be specified in advance. Certainly there is some arbitrariness in asking the planners to stipulate in advance the post-terminal rate or rates of growth in consumption which are to be achieved. But the procedure provides one explicit method of treating such arbitrariness, which is always involved in planning models with finite time horizons.[1]

There are other ways of specifying terminal conditions. They may in some part be set by a 'political' process: so many steel mills, so much aluminium capacity, self-sufficiency in particular lines of production. One way or another, however, they must in this type of model be established.

(2) The second step is to specify the planning period. There is no analytic device which will permit one to pick the 'best' planning period on *a priori* grounds. Some of the relevant considerations have been discussed briefly in the paper entitled 'The Choice Elements in Intertemporal Planning'. These, however, are not completely economic in character.[1]

(3) In the third step a method of determining the level of consumption of the various items *within* the planning period must be settled upon. The method used in our earlier paper

[1] For a simple illustration of the logical intricacies involved in dealing with planning models over an infinite horizon see the paper by S. Chakravarty, 'The Existence of an Optimum Savings Programme', *Econometrica*, January 1962, and reproduced in the present volume.

[2] In this, as in the planning frameworks to be discussed later, application of the model over different planning periods raises different problems of estimation of empirical parameters and of projection of terminal conditions. The logic of the models does not change with the planning period so long as it remains finite. It is true, however, that the quantitative results will be sensitive to changes in the length of the horizon.

requires the exogenous determination of the rate of growth of consumption in each sector. This can be a single number, so that consumption of all items is guaranteed to grow at the same rate, or different consumption growth rates can be specified for each sector. The determination of the different growth rates is a matter outside the analytical boundaries of the model itself. If this procedure appears arbitrary then consumption can be just as well treated endogenously by means of consumption-income relations for the various sectors. In the latter procedure the model becomes 'closed' with respect to consumption, and the path of development is constrained by private consumption patterns. In this case, however, we lose our freedom to posit any set of terminal conditions, and the terminal positions must be worked out from the model.

It is equally possible, and perhaps closer to reality, to regard some consumption patterns, e.g. in food grains and textiles, as in fact constraining the pattern of development and the consumption of other items, e.g. automobiles and housing, as subject to the exogenous determination and control of specific policies. The existence of endogenous consumption-income relationships of a sub-set of commodities and sectors would limit the number of terminal conditions which can be stipulated in advance.

(4) Finally, after all the previous steps have been taken the 'problem' can be solved. The problem is to determine the initial levels of consumption and subsequent levels of output, consumption, and investment in each sector in each period which are consistent with the decisions taken in the first three steps relating to final targets, the planning period, and consumption behaviour.

Solutions for the differential as well as the difference equation formulation of the model have been worked out, that is for continuous as well as discreet time progression, and for uniform as well as non-uniform exogenously specified rates of growth of consumption.[1] The analytic framework presented in the preceding chapter shows that, given the targets, the planning period, and the intermediate consumption behaviour, we can

---

[1] If there are extended and different gestation lags of investment in the various sectors, the analytical and computational problems become somewhat more involved but are not essential barriers to a solution.

find initial and subsequent levels of consumption, investment, and output which are consistent.

It should be clear, however, that in this formulation the burden of adjustment necessary to achieve consistency is thrown on the initial levels of consumption. These are not 'givens'; they are not taken from what has been observed at the start of the planning period. They are derived as a consequence of the choice of the other elements which are made. Will that 'burden' of adjustment be a difficult one? Would the changes required be 'politically' feasible? If they are not, what changes in the other elements would produce initial consumption levels which are realistic? These most significant questions cannot be answered by *a priori* reasoning. They depend not just on the structure of the analytic framework but on the numerical values of the parameters as well as the values given to the choice elements. The answers must wait, therefore, on the numerical trial of this model.

Of course there are other formulations of this basic idea of a consistency model which would adapt themselves to the political fact, such as it is, that initial levels of consumption cannot be changed, or cannot be changed much, or, more precisely, can only be changed by amounts which the planner could specify. If initial consumption levels become 'givens', then the 'free' variables must be either the intermediate growth rates in consumption or the terminal conditions. To the extent that consumption of certain commodities is determined by income elasticities or Engel equations, these items are not completely free to adjust if initial and terminal conditions are fixed. The entire burden of adjustment then is thrown on just those 'free' consumption items, say, automobiles and housing. Again, however, it remains a practical question which could be decided only by numerical trials as to whether this would provide sufficient flexibility.

There is another question regarding this latter formulation as to the feasibility of solution. When the unknowns in the problem are each of the intermediate consumption growth rates, the mathematical difficulties seem to be substantially increased. This, however, requires still further exploration.

Still another alternative formulation is to let the terminal conditions be the 'free' variables with initial conditions taken at whatever they happen to be and to have the intermediate consumption levels determined by endogenous relations or exogenous specification, whichever is considered more realistic and tractable. In this formulation the planning framework becomes a 'projection' model. The purpose of working out the whole thing is to see what these specifications imply about the future. The 'targets' for the end of the planning period cannot be set exogenously. They are an implication of the model which must be worked out in order to see where the economy is going and where it will be at the end of the planning period. The terminal consumption levels and investment levels and the post-terminal growth rates are not chosen beforehand but are implications of the working out of the system itself. They are calculated after everything else is set.

In this as in the other formulations of the 'consistency' model there can be trials to determine the implications of alternative stipulations of conditions for the model. In the 'projection' version these trials would demonstrate the alternative patterns of growth in each sector and final levels of production which would be achieved. The planners could then choose that option which is considered most satisfactory.

In each of these formulations of a 'consistency' model, the generalization from a single sector or aggregated one good version to a many sector framework is relatively straight-forward. It is for many purposes quite possible to think in terms of the aggregated version and generalize the conclusions to many sectors. Naturally the generalization is not always obvious and may miss certain essential problems.

In the many sector version the question arises as to whether the condition of 'non-negativity' is preserved for all the variables. Mathematical consistency which requires that some sectors operate at negative output levels or some capital stocks be run down below zero is not acceptable economics. It is not necessary and it may not even be desirable to impose the condition that all investment levels be non-negative as well. This would commit the economy to maintain capital stocks in every sector even when its preferences may have changed.

Non-negativity of output and capital stock variables cannot always be guaranteed in this type of consistency model although

143

situations in which negativity troubles will not arise can be specified in advance. Moreover, once all the necessary numbers are specified it can be ascertained by actual computation whether or not non-negativity is preserved. If negativity is a danger, an intervening period of adjustment to a safe set of initial conditions can be imagined. What a 'safe' set of initial conditions would be and whether or not they would also be 'politically feasible' are questions which must be answered by actually working out alternative solutions.

There are limits as to how far one can go in *a priori* specification of a 'consistency' model which can be guaranteed to be satisfactory to a planner. Though the details have not been worked out here and some problems require further work, the boundaries have been established. The only way of going beyond them is to begin to actually work the model and to analyse the results.

Suppose, for example, using the initial formulation of the 'consistency' model, terminal conditions were to be set for consumption and capital stock vectors. Then the behaviour of intermediate consumption in each sector is accounted for by stipulation in some sectors and Engel equations in other sectors. Doing all this implies that a considerable amount of empirical work has already been done on estimation of parameters before one ever tries to work the planning model. It is not easy work but feasible, given enough effort and resources. The next step is to solve the problem and find the initial conditions and path of output, consumption, and investment implied. Only at this point can it be determined whether the condition of non-negativity, for example, is met. Maybe it will be and it is not even a close question. It is tempting to say that would be lucky, but it is not a matter of luck. The answer is all there in the numbers and planning framework and just has to be worked out. Once past that hurdle, the initial consumption conditions implied are examined and compared with those actually in existence at the beginning of the planning period. The comparison may be close, so that this implication of the plan is judged to be 'politically' feasible and the other implications can be inspected. Even if it all 'passed' on political as well as economic feasibility grounds, a re-run would be ordered immediately in order to determine whether a change in the terminal or intermediate conditions would lead to results which were both feasible and politically even more desirable.

Of course the results might not 'pass'. There may be troubles due to negativity, and the derived initial levels of consumption may be impossibly different from the prevailing ones. So again the terminal conditions would have to be adjusted and a new, perhaps more acceptable, solution found. The trials and re-trials would not have to be 'blind'. A programme of experimentation might be developed to explore alternatives. But the alternatives would have to be explored empirically as purely deductive efforts alone would not yield full answers to the empirical questions asked. Though logically the amount of empirical exploration possible is endless, the actual amount necessary for planning purposes need not turn out to be so great. The problem, though a big one, seems well within the capacity of modern computing machines to solve many times and relatively quickly. That is what must be done in order to develop a useful planning framework.

II. THE FULLY OPTIMIZING APPROACH

A fully optimizing model has an appeal which cannot be matched by any less ambitious framework. It attempts to find the 'best' possible pattern of resource allocation over time and among sectors. The 'best' is understood in the sense of maximization of a stipulated preference function involving the relevant dated variables. So, if an optimal programme can be established, the attempt to do as well as possible has succeeded; the goal has been achieved, and the planner can sit back with a justified sense of satisfaction.

In attaining all this, a fully optimizing model will also elimin-ate those worries about the possible negativity of solutions which may bother a planner using a consistency model. This will be a result of the inequalities which are built into the structure and which keep the system at least at non-negative levels of output in all the sectors. As regards initial conditions, these can be included in the set of constraints which characterize the model. Or, alternatively, they can be included among the unknowns which will be determined by the solution to the intertemporal maximization problem.

Without giving a fully optimizing model in detail an outline will be presented of the main steps involved in constructing such a planning framework.

(1) The first step is to decide on what it is which will be optimized and into what type of preference function the variables will enter. Any variety of things could be optimized though not all choices are equivalent in terms of the economic opportunities they provide. Just two possibilities will be considered here.

(a) Given some terminal capital stocks as well as initial capital stocks, the planning framework might be asked to optimize with respect to some specified utility function which includes all the various consumption items in each year of the planning period. The terminal capital stocks could be determined in such a way as to guarantee a particular rate of equiproportional growth or a vector of growth rates for the different sectors in the post-terminal period. The planned initial levels of consumption could be constrained to be at just those actually prevailing or at other levels chosen by the planner. Likewise it would be possible to set, on exogenous policy grounds, consumption of particular items at predetermined levels and to maximize the utility to be gained from all other consumption goods. For analytic and computational manageability the utility function chosen should have a linear form. However, economically this is quite a restrictive assumption. It implies a constancy of the marginal utility of consumption with respect to each consumption item for any period of time.

(b) Or it would be possible to specify some linear behaviour relations for consumption goods and for given initial levels of capacity. Optimization could then be carried out with respect to some preference function of terminal capital stocks. This function likewise ought to be linear in form to insure analytic and computational feasibility. In this case the terminal condition targets and the potential post-terminal growth rates could not be known until there were a solution to the planning problem.

(c) Most inter-temporal linear programming models are bound to rely on the choice of one or another set of constant preference coefficients which of course cannot avoid being arbitrary. It is logically possible to formulate the planning problem as a non-linear problem, where the implied preference function may have a greater degree of intuitive significance. If we formulate the planning problem as one minimizing the time needed to transform a given set of initial conditions to a desired set of terminal goals, then the problem assumes a non-linear character. Thus, if the initial conditions are written as a vector X(0) and the desired terminal conditions as a vector X(T), the rate of change of X with respect to time t is

$$\frac{dX}{dt} = f[X(t), y(t), t],$$

where y(t) is a set of decision variables referring to time t and is a vector valued function of vectors. With a model of constant coefficients type t will not figure as an independent variable.

Thus for a dynamic model of the Leontief type

$$B\frac{dX}{dt} = (I - A)X(t) - C(t)$$

or

$$\frac{dX}{dt} = B^{-1}(I - A)X(t) - B^{-1}C(t)$$

where B is assumed to be irreducible and B^{-1} exists. The problem, then, is to choose C(t) in such a way as to minimize the time needed to transform X(0) into X(T). Additional restrictions on the non-negativity of the solution or inequalities of the form $C(t) \geq \bar{C}$ may be imposed. This type of optimization problem with inequalities added as a side condition, however, has a number of special difficulties in obtaining a solution.

(2) Having stipulated the form of the model and the constraints desired, the next step is to work out the solution. Intersectoral and inter-temporal consistency are automatically assured from the method of setting up and solving the problem and the result is sure to be the 'best' possible one.

Once having that result, however, the planner can by no means rest on his laurels but must immediately begin recomputing for alternative specifications of the consumption utility

K*

function or the terminal stock preference function, depending on the formulation used. There is no way of knowing what the coefficients of a national utility or preference function are, but we can be sure that the planning results will be sensitive to those coefficients. For example, if all the relevant relationships are linear, as they are nearly always assumed to be for computational tractability, the set of solutions satisfying all the inequalities for each time period span a solution space of very high dimensionality with a lot of 'corners'. Any optimal solution will be at one of the corners or will be a convex combination of some of the corner conditions. Changing one or more of the coefficients of the utility or preference function is like shifting the weights on a board resting on an irregular pile of rocks. The board will move and come to rest somewhere else. What will be the new solution? It is not possible to provide an answer on *a priori* grounds. One must just try to see what the results are.

Trying the model for many different combinations of the coefficients of the utility or preference functions is a big job which will yield information about the sensitivity of the results to changes in these coefficients. Suppose the results are not sensitive to 'small' changes and are sensitive to 'big' changes. What then? There is still no basis for a firm idea as to what these coefficients are. Perhaps by taking a 'fresh look' at the different results a planner might decide which he liked best.

In the fully optimizing model, as in the consistency model, the framework, data requirements, and character of the results are closely related. If it is the utility of consumption over the entire planning period which is optimized with stipulated terminal stocks, all the problems of stipulating the terminal stocks emerge as in the previous planning frameworks *and* there is the additional requirement of specifying a utility function which includes all the different consumption items. If it is a preference function of terminal capital stocks which is optimized with consumption stipulated exogenously or by means of Engel equations, or both, then as in the projection version of the consistency model the terminal state of the economy and the potential post-terminal growth rates will be determined only in the process of solving the model.

In fully optimizing models we are not committed to a policy

of full utilization of capacity in each sector in each period. However, it is doubtful whether an optimal solution will deviate significantly from the no-excess capacity pattern provided that we assume final demand for each sector to increase and that a meaningful solution exists on the no-excess capacity assumption.

III. SUMMARY

The difficulties in applying multi-sector, inter-temporal planning frameworks are essential difficulties which arise not from the model approach but from the inherent nature of the planning problem. These difficulties are only concealed or ignored in the usual procedures which plan with an aggregate income concept or ignore the requirements of inter-sectoral consistency or are restricted to static consistency requirements. Certainly any opinion which regards the difficulties of applying multi-sector, inter-temporal planning models as faults rather than virtues is obscurantist.

In turn this does not imply that the proper planner must instantly embrace the most sophisticated and fully developed optimizing framework to establish himself firmly on the side of human progress and enlightenment. There are tactics of planning as well as grand strategy. What are the criteria for a tactical choice among the alternative approaches described above? The following two are suggested:

(1) The planning framework must be understandable to those persons on whom the burden of economic decisions falls. This, to be sure, is not a clear-cut criterion. The least common denominator in understanding should not be controlling; neither should the professional economist specialist in planning techniques dictate the terms in which planning is to be done. The specialist must lead but not by so far as to lose contact with those for whom he is working. This can only be a matter of judgment. It is a matter which deserves careful thought because planning models whose general structure is not understandable to decision-makers are for them a waste of time and have no chance of application.

(2) The planning framework suggested must have 'good' chances of success. That is, it should offer results which represent

149

additions to knowledge as compared to the results achieved by the currently used techniques. In addition, these results must also be attainable within a 'reasonable' span of time. It is no good offering results only after 'perfect' data and 'perfect' planning models are available.

This criterion should not be so hard to meet. The explicit, multi-sectoral, inter-temporal planning models should have at least the data and sense of any less sophisticated method. Even if the results of a fully specified multi-sector planning model only verified currently used, less sophisticated methods, that in itself would represent an addition to knowledge which would be worth the effort unless someone could predict with certainty that outcome in advance. Certainly the results should not lead to error and represent a subtraction from wisdom. That could happen if the quality of information and judgment used in an explicit planning framework were less good than otherwise available and practiced and yet the former were allowed to prevail. In a planning organization open to diverse points of view that seems to be an unlikely outcome.

The conclusion to be drawn from this survey seems to be that none of the types of models considered can be so fully and adequately specified in advance that they can be fed into a computer which in turn will proceed to grind out the next Five or Twenty Year Plan. A series of actual trials with alternative numbers for targets, preference functions, consumption behaviour relations, initial conditions, and so on must be an essential part of the process of developing a planning framework whatever formal planning structure is used. This may be a disappointment, but it does not imply that intertemporal multi-sector planning cannot be done or that it is useless if attempted. It does mean that there is another important step in the development of planning models between writing down an analytical framework and obtaining results which can be implemented.

10

THE EXISTENCE OF AN
OPTIMUM SAVINGS PROGRAMME

S. CHAKRAVARTY[1]

I

The purpose of this chapter is to analyse critically the nature of the solutions that have been offered to the problem of how much a nation should optimally save. Since savings in this connection is the only alternative to consumption, this is equivalent to the problem of how much a nation should optimally consume. An optimal consumption programme is one that makes a certain stipulated functional in utilities f(U(c(t))) as high as possible, subject to certain restrictions on the class of admissible utility and production functions. U here is an indicator of instantaneous utility and C(t) is consumption at point t.

Two approaches have been adopted in finding this optimal programme: (*a*) to define the functions C(t) on a finite time interval $(0 \leq t \leq T)$ which corresponds to a finite planning horizon. This makes the domain of the functions closed and bounded. Together with the assumption of continuity of the various functions, this is in principle enough to solve the problem of the optimal programme over the relevant time horizon. But the solution may be crucially dependent on the length of time period T and the valuation attached to the terminal stock of capital.[2]

---

[1] This was written during the author's stay at the Massachusetts Institute of Technology as a Visiting Assistant Professor of Economics.

My original interest in the problem is due to Professor J. Tinbergen, who has also been kind enough to favour me with comments on the present paper. In the present formulation of the problem, I have benefited greatly from the comments made by Professors R. M. Solow and P. A. Samuelson on earlier drafts of the chapter and from discussions with Professor P. N. Rosenstein-Rodan. In addition, Messrs R. A. Gangolli, S. A. Marglin, and Professors John H. Kareken, R. S. Eckaus and Louis Lefeber have provided valuable comments. (Originally published in *Econometrica*, January 1962.)

[2] Some recent work done by the present author seems to indicate, however, that with a functional criterion of maximizing $\int_0^T U(t)dt$, the extremals defining

151

The latter is not a meaningful concept unless we try to take into account what happens beyond T. This reveals the problem essentially as extending indefinitely over t. To tackle this problem of indefinite extension in time an alternative formulation is presented: (b) the functions C(t) are now defined for any t > 0, i.e. the time horizon is infinite. The domain is no longer compact. To choose the optimal consumption programme in this case, it is necessary to formulate the problem in such a way that an ordering is introduced on the functions characterizing alternative policies with regard to consumption. This requirement is obvious since, without an order, there is no way of defining the best programme. It is the contention of this paper that the attempts in the literature up to date either do not pay sufficient attention to introducing this order and thus fail in properly formulating the problem, or they do so in an arbitrary way, which ensures mathematical tractability but little more.[1] The demonstration of this point emphasizes the necessity of more closely studying those features of infinite programmes that enable us to discriminate among them without being totally dependent on one or the other arbitrary assumption. It should be noted that the choice problem is here posed in a nonstochastic context. Introducing a discount factor reflecting uncertainty of the future, while facilitating certain questions regarding infinity of time, would introduce many other complications which obviously do not fall within the scope of the problem discussed here.

II

The *locus classicus* of this problem is to be found in the 1928 paper of Ramsey on the mathematical theory of savings [5]. Subsequently, the following have been the noteworthy contributions to the problem: (a) the work of Samuelson and Solow [6] in extending Ramsey's analysis to a world involving multiple

---

the best policy are not significantly sensitive to changes in the terminal capital stock as against changes in the length of the horizon. See S. Chakravarty, 'Optimal Savings with Finite Horizon', CENIS, Massachusetts Institute of Technology, March 1961, published in the *International Economic Review*, September 1962.

[1] Mathematically, the root of the difficulty in case (b) is in the absence of compactness of the policy space. For the real line, compactness is the same as closedness and boundedness.

capital goods; (b) the recent papers of Tinbergen [8, 9] which do not adopt the specific Ramsey assumption of a finite 'bliss' defined as a maximum conceivable state of satisfaction but are essentially concerned with discovering the policy implications of a one-commodity capital model by using 'econometrically tested' utility and production functions; and (c) the papers by Stone [7] and Meade [4] who made strictly Ramsey-type assumptions but tried to uncover the policy implications for aggregative, but more specific, situations characterized by explicit production and utility functions. In the last thirty years, these have been the major contributions to a subject whose fascination is matched only by its difficulties. In our discussion we shall be primarily concerned with the results of Ramsey and Tinbergen, because the nature of the difficulties involved in selecting a best consumption programme over an infinite time comes out very clearly in these one-commodity models. In a disaggregated model, the same difficulties would persist, fortified by additional complications.

Somewhat different in spirit but bearing essentially on the same problem, we have the remarkable contributions of Malinvaud [3] and Koopmans [2] on which we shall have occasion to comment briefly.

III

While the contributions mentioned above have been primarily positive, at least in intention, there have been critics who have sought to dismiss the problem as being an exercise with little significance for theory and none for policy-making whatsoever [1]. I feel that there are two reasons why such criticism may not be very well taken.

First, the main analytical interest of these models consists in their attempt to tackle certain issues at the heart of the theory of capital, such as the question of horizon involved in discussions of intertemporal allocation of scarce resources. Merely to say that the problem is settled in practice by a political decision is not to say that the problem does not exist or that a procedure is indicated as to how to resolve the conceptual difficulties. It only amounts to a confession of failure, without trying to analyse what the failure is due to.

Secondly, from the policy point of view, the importance of the problem should not be underrated. Assume for the time being that we have one central decision-maker who is interested in drawing up a savings plan over time. The preference ordering of such a decision-maker *need* not be represented by a cardinal utility function, but it would simplify discussion if we assume cardinal utility.[1] Then, the Ramsey-Tinbergen problem is placed in its proper setting and whenever this setting applies even in a rough way, the resulting analysis will apply.

The discussion of this question becomes all the more important if, following Tinbergen, one assumes that there is a consecutiveness in policy decisions as to permit a splitting up of the problem of resource allocation into conceptually different *stages*. Mathematically, such a decomposition corresponds roughly to the notion of block-triangularity of the coefficients matrix in linear decision problems. Thus, a decision on how much the nation should optimally save is followed by the optimal distribution of the savings between the different sectors of the economy. In this way, broad macroeconomic conclusions can be derived without entering into details to start with.

IV

Let us consider Tinbergen's papers first. His first paper had a somewhat restricted scope in view; he was concerned with finding a savings ratio which would be optimal for all future years, given the utility and production functions, and the initial endowment of capital. He also assumed a subjective rate of time preference, independent of diminishing utility or uncertainty. His problem, then, was to maximize the integral of discounted utility over time with respect to a parameter, e.g. the savings ratio. This is a very restricted problem and Tinbergen himself was well aware of it. The restriction arises from considering only programmes with fixed savings ratios. But what is optimal among this class of programmes would not be optimal in the sense of maximizing an integral of discounted

---

[1] That uniqueness up to a linear transformation is being assumed in this case is clear from the fact that both Ramsey and Tinbergen are concerned with finding policies which maximize an integral of utility over a period of time. Discussions by Malinvaud and Koopmans are free from this restrictive assumption.

utilities over time. Properly formulated, the problem is one in the variational calculus. This is what Tinbergen does in his *Econometrica* article. Thus, we have the following problem:

Max $\int_0^\infty U[C(t)]dt$ subject to $C(t) = bK(t) - \dot{K}(t)$ where b is the average and marginal output-capital ratio, here assumed to be constant, $U(C) > 0$, $U'(C) \geq 0$, $U''(C) < 0$, and $K(0)$ is given. It is seen that the functional in Tinbergen's case is an improper integral. Thus the question of the best choice of a savings programme can only arise in this form if a preliminary property is verified, namely that the stipulated functional has a maximum. Since the functional in this case is an integral over an unbounded range, the question boils down to an even more preliminary one, e.g. the question of its convergence on our previous specifications of the utility and production functions.

The economic significance of formulating the choice problem as one of maximizing $\int_0^\infty Udt$ arises from the possible ordering that the functional imposes on alternative infinite programmes. But if the total utility associated with any feasible infinite programme is infinitely large, because $\int_0^\infty Udt$ does not converge, then there is no possibility of introducing any order on the policy space through such mappings from the policy to the utility space. Except in the sense of pointwise dominance, such a functional $\int_0^\infty Udt$ does not discriminate among alternative programmes and hence defines an economically uninteresting mapping. Pointwise dominance is patently a special case and cannot be assumed on an *a priori* basis.[1]

[1] Malinvaud has suggested an interesting procedure to compare alternative infinite programmes, each of which gives infinite satisfaction. Thus, in Orwellian language, all infinite programmes are equal, but some are more equal than the others. So far as I can see, Malinvaud's procedure consists in dividing the class of feasible infinite programmes into two sub-classes, (a) programmes that differ only for a number of periods T, where T is arbitrary and finite, but are identical afterwards; (b) all the other programmes that are feasible. Now for a given T, the programmes belonging to (a) are comparable among themselves and the one giving the highest value of the functional up to T should be chosen. By making T arbitrarily large, we widen the set of admissible programmes and so long as T remains finite, however large, a best programme exists among programmes admitted.

This procedure, while extremely interesting, hinges on the crucial assumption that letting $T \to \infty$, the various best programmes (best for each choice of T) will tend to 'the best programme'. If this does not hold, then the procedure suggested by Malinvaud does not work but it must still be granted that Malinvaud's procedure provides us with necessary conditions for determining the best programme in the infinite dimensional policy space.

Returning to Tinbergen's problem, it may be useful to divide the class of admissible utility functions into two sub-classes: (a) the functions U(C) which do not admit a bliss point; (b) the functions admitting a bliss point. What the existence of bliss implies is that as consumption grows larger and larger over time, the utility associated with this consumption has a finite upper bound. It may, however, be profitable to distinguish further under (b) three sub-cases:

(i) There is a finite level of consumption corresponding to this upper bound on the utility function.

(ii) There is no finite level of consumption which corresponds to the upper bound on the utility function but there is an asymptotic approach towards the upper bound with consumption increasing. An example of (ii) is given by the hyperbolic utility function given in Tinbergen [8]: $U(C) = U_0(1 - c^0/C)$. Here the upper bound U_0 is never attained but only approached as $C \to \infty$. The function is only defined for the constant $c^0 > 0$.

(iii) In this case, not only is there a finite consumption which attains finite bliss, but to push consumption beyond this point lowers total utility. This is the saturation case mentioned by Tinbergen [8] towards the end of his paper. This case is improper for our present discussion, because it implies $U'C < 0$, while we have assumed on general qualitative grounds that $U'(C) > 0$.

On assumption (a) which is Tinbergen's first example, $U(C(t))$ grows indefinitely with C increasing. One necessary condition for $\int_0^\infty U[C(t)]dt$ to converge is that $U(C(t)) \to 0$ as $t \to \infty$. If we assume a programme with C increasing over time, even if $U'(C) \to 0$, because of diminishing marginal utility, it does not follow that $U(t) \to 0$ with the passage of time. Thus the necessary condition for the convergence of the integral is not satisfied. Hence, the problem is not adequately formulated either from an economic or a mathematical point of view.

On assumptions (b) i, ii, which admit bliss, but rule out negative marginal utility for any level of consumption, $U[C(t)]$ tends towards the bliss level as $t \to \infty$. Thus, if $U_0 = B$ (bliss), then, once again, the integral $\int_0^\infty U[C(t)]dt$ does not converge for what tends to 0 is $[B - U(t)]$ and not $U(t)$.

Thus, on either set of assumptions, the functional is divergent and, therefore, no order can be introduced among the alternative paths through using the functional criterion $\int_0^\infty$ Udt. This implies that the problem of determining the best infinite programme is not properly posed with this particular choice of the functional.

In trying to maximize the integral $\int_0^\infty$ Udt, Tinbergen comes out with an optimal time path of consumption which turns out to be equal to the subsistence level of consumption. This apparently surprising result is due to the fact that we are considering as the functional the undiscounted sum of utilities over an *infinite* period. With Tinbergen's assumptions of a constant marginal productivity of capital and a very slow decline in marginal utility of consumption, it can never pay to consume anything more than the minimum, because what we lose by not consuming today will be made up by what we gain from the satisfaction due to the extra product over an infinite time. Thus, if there were no restriction on minimum consumption, which merely reflects an arbitrary choice of origin, the rule would have been to save 100 per cent, inasmuch as, however much one reduces consumption, the marginal utility of consumption never increases enough to equal the marginal utility of savings for any positive level of consumption. Thus, savings is always more worthwhile, till one reaches the corner situation where everything is saved. This result is the reflection of the fact that the integral $\int_0^\infty$ Udt is divergent and therefore rules out a maximal solution in the usual sense.

A precise way of looking at this problem would be to maximize the integral of utility over a finite time, T, and then, letting T become infinitely large, see what turns out to be the programme over an infinite period. Thus, the problem is now to maximize $\int_0^T$ U[C(t)]dt, for a pre-assigned finite T. This is a well behaved problem subject to our specifications on the utility and production functions. Assume that $C_T(t)$ maximizes this integral for $t \le T$. With a change in the upper bound from T to $T' \neq T$, we shall then have another maximizing function $C_{T'}(t)$ defined for $t \le T'$. The problem max $\int_0^\infty$ Udt has a meaningful solution if and only if the functions $C_T(t)$ tend to a limit function $C\infty(t)$ as $T \to \infty$ which maximizes the above improper integral.

We have, therefore, to investigate two problems: (*a*) whether

157

the limit function exists, e.g. test whether $\lim_{T\to\infty} C_T(t) = C_\infty(t)$, a definite function; (*b*) if the limit function exists, whether there is a sense in which it maximizes the integral $\int_0^\infty$ Udt. We have, however, already seen that in the present case $\int_0^\infty$ U[C(t)]dt is clearly divergent. Thus, it is not meaningful to talk of a maximum here in the sense of a maximizing solution to a customary variational problem. It may, however, so happen that there exists a maximal solution in the sense that it pointwise dominates all other functions from a certain time onwards. It is only in this latter sense that one should try to assess whether the limit function constitutes a maximum in the function space.

With Tinbergen's specifications on the relevant functions, which include a constant marginal productivity of capital, *b*, and a marginal utility function $dU/dc = (C_t - \bar{C})^{-v}$, $v < 1$, it is easy to show that the limit function exists but does not constitute a maximum in any sense. To prove this, take the problem: max $\int_0^T$ Udt with initial condition $K_T(0) = K_o$, the initial amount of capital-stock, and boundary condition $\dot{K}_T = 0$, implying that we consume the entire income in the last period. For this specific problem, we get the following extremal path for K by using the conventional variational procedure:

$$K(t) = Ae^{bt} + Be^{(b/v)t}$$

where $A = K_o - B$, $B = K_o / (1 - \frac{1}{v}e^{b\frac{(1-v)}{v}T})$.

It is easy to see that as $T \to \infty$, $B \to 0$. This means that $\lim_{T\to\infty} K_T(t) \to K_o e^{bt}$. This implies that the limiting path for consumption, $\lim_{T\to\infty} C_T(t)$, approaches 0, if there is no lower bound on consumption. If we assume a non-zero subsistence level of consumption, as on grounds of realism one ought to, then we have $\lim_{T\to\infty} C_T(t) \to \bar{C}$. But the choice of this subsistence level as mentioned previously implies a mere translation and in no way affects the nature of the problem. It is, however, clear that for T finite, C(t) >0, or $>\bar{C}$, as the case may be, but, in the limit, consumption is being indefinitely postponed.

Whether the limit function constitutes a maximum is now the crucial point. This point is easily decided because we may easily construct another function C(t)>0, satisfying the initial conditions as above which dominates the limit function pointwise. Thus, the limit function cannot constitute a maximum,

158

because it is dominated by another admissible function. Whether the limit function constitutes a minimum in general depends on introducing a suitable order for this purpose. In the present case, however, this happens to constitute a minimum on any relevant definition of order because it is the only admissible programme that is mapped to zero by the functional $\int_0^\infty U dt$, while all other admissible functions are mapped to infinity. This result is also intuitively obvious when one realizes that at any single point of time only the minimum utility is being enjoyed and because of the shifting time-horizon, the day for enjoying the fruits of saving never arrives. It therefore appears that Tinbergen's procedure, while valid for a finite horizon, breaks down when we let the horizon extend indefinitely in time.

V

Ramsey, however, had a different functional in mind, namely (minimize) $\int_0^\infty [B - U(C(t))]dt$. In this case, the utility function is always bounded above by a maximum conceivable state of satisfaction, Bliss, denoted by B. The relevant question in this connection is whether this level B is attained for a finite level of consumption or whether there is merely an asymptotic approach towards B. In the first case the functional $\int_0^\infty [B - U(C(t))]dt$ defines a meaningful order and we may work out the best savings programme in the light of this order. But in the second situation, where Bliss is that approached asymptotically, we may still run into difficulties because the functional may not define a nondiscriminatory mapping from the policy to the utility space.

The following example illustrates this point. Take the case of the hyperbolic utility function, $U(C) = U_0(1 - c^\circ/C)$, where $U_0 = $ Bliss. Then, we have

$$\int_0^\infty \left[U_0 - U_0\left(1 - \frac{c^\circ}{C(t)}\right) \right] dt = \int_0^\infty \frac{U_0 c^\circ}{C(t)} dt.$$

Now, for $C(t) = \bar{C}$, this integral does not converge. Thus, a constant consumption programme is ruled out. This is trivial from the economic point of view. But suppose that $C(t) = C_0 + \propto t$ then, also, the integral does not converge. Here consumption is growing linearly but $\int_0^\infty (1/t)dt$ is divergent. Our qualitative specifications on the production function do not, however, rule out the case of systems whose most rapid rate of growth of consumption is linear, and that is interesting.[1]

The point of the above discussion is that even in this modified Ramsey case, if there is no finite level of consumption corresponding to Bliss, the usual qualitative restrictions on the utility function and production function do not rule out the possibility that a meaningful solution may fail to exist. It may be that empirical restrictions on parameters of production functions are such that the linear or logarithmic growth case is always ruled out in practice. But then the problem is an empirical one and not a purely logical one, a possibility not at all envisaged by Ramsey himself.

VI

Another answer, which has been proposed to this question, is to introduce a subjective rate of time preference. Then the functional is not the integral of utility over time but the integral of discounted utility of consumption over time, where the rate of discount is a pure rate of time preference.[2] Tinbergen himself had used these specifications in his first paper, with the added restriction that the savings rate be a constant. Now, in the variational case we have Max $\int_0^\infty U(C) \, e^{-Pt} \, dt$ subject to $C(t) = bK(t) - \dot{K}(t)$ or $C(t) = K^P - \dot{K}(t)$, $P < 1$, if we assume a simple Cobb-Douglas production function.

Even here, the functional is bounded above only if the combined effects of diminishing marginal utility and time preference relative to the rate of growth of consumption are such as to satisfy the convergence conditions. To assume that such conditions will always be satisfied is an instance of implicit theorizing, because we assume that a certain inequality between the productivity coefficient, the coefficient of the elasticity of marginal utility and time preference would always be satisfied in such a way as to give us the desired solution.

Alternatively, if a continuous non-trivial ordering of infinite

[1] What would be true of a linear growth rate would also be true, *a fortiori*, of a system growing logarithmically with time.

[2] The 'pure rate of time preference' may have to be distinguished from the notion of a 'social rate of time preference', based on any consideration relating to equity between generations.

consumption programmes exists, this, under certain assumed conditions relating to sensitivity, stationarity, and periodwise aggregation, may be interpreted as implying the existence of a time perspective. This refers to the result[1] which Koopmans obtained in his recent paper [2] about impatience being logically implied in a utility function of an infinite consumption programme. It should be carefully noted that Koopmans derives time preference as a *consequence*, rather than as an *empirically testable* hypothesis, as has been the general tradition in the literature on capital theory. The importance of the Koopmans theorem may not be fully understood if we restrict our thinking of a utility functional to one necessarily representable by an integral of instantaneous utilities. In fact, Koopmans' result includes a much wider class of functionals of which the integral formulation is a special case.

VII

The upshot of the above discussion has been to indicate that the various optimal infinite programmes that have been discussed in the literature suffer from either an improper formulation which may render the solutions economically irrelevant, or from the restrictiveness that arises from crucial dependences on certain arbitrary assumptions. A functional criterion such as Max $\int_0^\infty U dt$ does not impose any ordering on the policy space, except in the sense of pointwise dominance, because with the usual qualitative specifications on the admissible utility and production functions, the integral does not converge, and thus the results obtained from this procedure in these cases are not economically meaningful. On the other hand, functional criteria such as Min $\int_0^\infty (B-U)dt$, where B is reached for a finite consumption, or Max $\int_0^\infty e^{-Pt} U(t)dt$ impose some ordering on the utility space, but they do it in completely arbitrary ways.[2]

---

[1] It is, however, useful to point out that the above results of Koopmans is not always necessary to obtain a continuous non-trivial ordering of alternative infinite programmes, because if we take the Ramsey case of a finite level of consumption which attains Bliss, there is no necessity for assuming time preference even though a best programme exists and, therefore, *a fortiori*, an order.

[2] Compare the following statement by Graaff on time-preference: 'Until someone suggests a way in which an observable choice can be made between "*n* units of present utility and one unit of utility tomorrow", we cannot speak of *time-preference*. We can, of course, speak of an "intertemporal rate of substitution"—

In a sense, such arbitrary preference orderings are operationally meaningless statements so long as we do not have any method of refuting them. Since our interest lies primarily in the meaningfulness of the order introduced and not only in the mathematical requirements of introducing such order, one cannot avoid feeling that such formulations have very little significance apart from ensuring solvability of the mathematical problem of maximizing a functional $\int_0^\infty U dt$ subject to an initial condition.

REFERENCES

1. GRAAFF, J. V. D.: *Theoretical Welfare Economics*, Cambridge University Press, 1957.
2. KOOPMANS, T. C.: 'Utility and Impatience', *Econometrica*, April 1960.
3. MALINVAUD, E.: 'Capital Accumulation and Efficient Allocation of Resources', *Econometrica*, 1953.
4. MEADE, J. E.: 'Trade and Welfare', *Mathematical Appendix*, Oxford University Press, 1955.
5. RAMSEY, F. P.: 'A Mathematical Theory of Savings', *Economic Journal* December 1928.
6. SAMUELSON, P. A., and R. M. SOLOW: 'A Complete Capital Model Involving Heterogeneous Capital Goods,' *Quarterly Journal of Economics*, November 1956.
7. STONE, J. R.: 'Misery and Bliss', *Economia Internazionale*, 1955.
8. TINBERGEN, J.: 'The Optimum Rate of Savings', *Economic Journal*, 1956.
9. ———: 'Maximization of Utility over Time', *Econometrica*, April 1960.

the additional amount of a good a man must get today to compensate for a unit less tomorrow—but that is something quite different' (*Theoretical Welfare Economics*, p. 40).

INDEX

163